MAYHEM

CURTIS PARSONS

outskirts
press

Outskirts Press, Inc.
http://www.outskirtspress.com

ISBN: 978-1-9772-3339-4

Library of Congress Control Number: 2020923231

Cover Photo © 2021 www.gettyimages.com. All rights reserved - used with permission.

Outskirts Press and the "OP" logo are trademarks belonging to Outskirts Press, Inc.

PRINTED IN THE UNITED STATES OF AMERICA

TABLE OF CONTENTS

About the Author

Curtis Parsons spent forty years in public safety, which included law enforcement, fire-rescue, and emergency medical services. During his years in the fire service, he acquired certifications and licenses as an EMT-Specialist, firefighter instructor, NFPA fire code inspector, fire cause and origin investigator, and SCUBA diver. He retired from the fire department in 2007 as Assistant Fire Chief with twenty-five years of service.

Upon his retirement from the fire service, he enrolled in graduate school and in 2009, at the age of fifty-seven, received a Master's Degree in Leadership with a concentration in emergency management and homeland security. While completing his Master's program he was selected by his County Board of Commissioners to head the Office of Emergency Management in late 2007, where he served until July of 2016. He was named the Professional Emergency Management Coordinator of the Year by the Michigan State Police in 2015. He received an appointment by former Michigan Governor Rick Snyder to serve on the state's Public Safety Communications

Interoperability Board. He was appointed to a National Homeland Security Council in 2010, which engages directly with the US Department of Homeland Security in providing input into Critical Infrastructure Protection Initiatives and Homeland Security Outreach programs for all levels of government. The council is comprised of professional practitioners from Emergency Management and Homeland Security from across the country. He served as a council representative for the Chemical Facilities and Dams and Levees Critical Infrastructure Protection Sectors. His colleagues elected him as their national chairperson and he served two consecutive terms. Upon announcement of his retirement, he was presented a certificate of appreciation for leadership and distinguished service by the US Department of Homeland Security in May of 2016.

Chapter 1

———◆———

MY STORIES FROM WORKING EMERGENCY SERVICES

IT HAS BEEN quite a ride serving in emergency services in various capacities over my lifetime. I have seen the wonderment of a new life come into the world and watched others take their last breath. Like many other first responders, I have memories of tragic events that are seared into my brain that I will never forget. This book is a collection of stories which I have been personally involved in, spanning my lifetime. Some stories you may find humorous, while others are tragic in nature. Information regarding names and many locations of events have been excluded out of respect for the patients, victims and their family members.

I never considered writing a book about my experiences but have been encouraged to do so by family members and close friends. The average person does not know what it's like to walk in the shoes of those of us who have served or are now serving in emergency services. It is my sincere hope that the reader can sense what we experience while serving as first responders in our local communities.

Chapter 2

CHICKENS GO TO SCHOOL

ONE FRIDAY EVENING while working for the police department, my partner and I were doing security checks on the district school buildings. We would do that to help ensure the facilities were secured for the weekend to prevent vandalism. My partner dropped me off behind the high school and drove to the opposite end of the complex. I walked up to the back of the building and saw a pickup truck next to the building. I hid behind a corner of the building to observe what was taking place. In the moonlight, I saw two young men throwing something from the back of the truck through an open cantilever window. I radioed my partner to return to my location and to come in quietly.

Within minutes, he was standing beside me in the shadows. The two young men were removing chickens from two wooden crates on the back of a pick-up truck and throwing them into a classroom through the open window. When they had completed their task, they climbed into the truck and started the engine. My partner and I stepped into view and shined our flashlights into their startled faces. We approached and instructed them to shut off the motor; they immediately complied. We obtained their drivers' licenses and asked them what they were doing. The two mischief-makers readily admitted to their dirty deed. My partner asked the two for home phone numbers so he could contact their respective parents and they reluctantly provided the information.

I said, "You know what, partner? I don't think this is necessary." The sheepish students looked somewhat bewildered and hopeful at my suggestion.

My partner asked, "What do you think we should do?"

I replied, "I don't think there is any need to get their parents involved. Let's contact the high school principal instead."

The boys' eyes went wide and they pleaded, "Please call our parents instead, don't call the principal!"

I said, "No, I think it is more appropriate to call the principal."

You could see the fear on their faces as they contemplated what the principal might do. I contacted our dispatch center and requested the principal join us behind the high school. The dispatcher confirmed that the principle was on his way. During the time that we stood there waiting, I could tell these young men wished they had never thought of pulling off such a stunt. A short time later, the principal drove up and got out of his car. He approached us and asked what was going on. I explained that we had observed the two young men throwing chickens through a window that they had opened.

He looked at the two frightened students and said, "Here

is what is going to happen. I am going unlock the room and turn on the lights and you are going to catch every one of those chickens and get them back into the crates. Then you are going to clean the classroom top to bottom, and remove all bird droppings and feathers from the floor and desk tops. The classroom will be sanitized and spotless when you're done. When you have cleaned the room to my satisfaction, you can go home and we'll discuss this further in my office on Monday morning."

Unfortunately, my partner and I were unable to hang around to watch what was surely to be a circus when those two tried to recapture the two dozen chickens they had released. They had learned a lesson the hard way that night, but I must admit, it was a very clever prank.

Chapter 3

THE FEELING OF HELPLESSNESS

ANYONE WHO HAS worked in emergency services will attest to one truth: When you report for your shift, you never know what you will be involved in before you finish it. The cards are dealt for you, and you play the cards you're dealt! My career ambition was to become a Michigan State Trooper. Unfortunately, during the time I applied, the Michigan State Police Academy was closed for a period of about two years due to a class action suit. The suit was brought about as a result of an EEO policy initiated by the state. During that time period, I began working as a police reservist for the township police department, acquiring training and experience. It was a small department consisting of part-time officers augmented with a few of reservists like myself.

The community was mainly a farming area. During the summer months it was a thriving tourist area. We had a large influx of summer residents who owned cottages on our many beautiful lakes and thousands of race fans who flocked into the area to enjoy one of the premier NASCAR racing facilities in the country. Summertime was very busy with all the activities taking place. Some, but not all, of our responsibilities were performing security checks on businesses and school systems, and property checks on homes of citizens who were away on vacation. We would take complaints, write reports, perform traffic surveillance, make an occasional arrest and make ourselves visible to members of the community.

It was the beginning of the Fourth of July holiday weekend and we were performing property checks when we received a radio call from our central dispatch center for a vehicle collision several miles outside of our jurisdiction. Since the location of the crash was on a state highway, I asked dispatch if there was a state unit available. She responded that we were the closest available unit. I acknowledged her radio traffic and we headed to the scene with lights and siren activated. As we arrived, we found that five vehicles were involved and immediately called for multiple ambulances and patrol units for traffic control. There were car parts and and broken glass all over the highway. In the darkness I heard calls for help; people were trapped in their cars, crying and screaming. I began to survey the scene with the aid of my flashlight and saw someone lying in the middle of the roadway. His face was covered in blood as a result of being thrown through the windshield of his vehicle. I quickly retrieved a clean handkerchief and placed it on his cheek and told him to hold it there and we had more help on the way. I turned to take in the scene and a feeling of helplessness swept over me. There were so many injured and I had no training to help ease their pain and suffering. We would find out later the cause of this incident was a result of the driver in one vehicle swerving to miss a deer. That car struck the second vehicle head-on in the oncoming lane, causing a chain reaction. Vehicles three, four and five collided into the first two. This incident injured a total of ten drivers and occupants. Injuries ranged from bumps, bruises to broken limbs, internal injuries and serious head wounds. We received assistance from sheriff's deputies, state troopers, fire-rescue and multiple transport units.

After clearing the scene, my partner and I drove to a nearby gas station to wash up and grab a cup of coffee. I told him about the feeling of helplessness I had on the scene and he said, "It's not our job to treat the injured. We just need to make sure the resources are provided by those who can."

I disagreed with his logic and said, "I think anyone who works the streets should have some training to be able to render aid to those we come across."

Over the summer, more events would occur which only further determined me to acquire training on how to provide emergency care. In September of that year, I enrolled in an EMT program at a nearby community college. In July of the following year, I successfully passed the state written and practical examinations and received my EMT license. From that moment on, I carried a first aid kit and felt confident to provide emergency care wherever I was. It was during this period that I began to feel I could make a difference working in rescue and EMS fields. Since I had earned my EMT license, the local fire chief asked me if I would like to attend race events at the race track in our jurisdiction. He said, "We can always use

EMTs during race week." I agreed and worked fire-rescue for two events. During these times I had many opportunities to utilize my newly acquired training.

At the end of the summer, the fire chief asked me to join the fire department. After some deliberation, I accepted a position with the fire department. For a few years I would work evening shifts with the police department, go home, get a shower and some much needed sleep, get up and head to the fire station for a day at the race track. It was about this time I realized that my passion was working in the fire and emergency medical services. I stopped pursuing a career in law enforcement and utilized every opportunity I was provided to increase my knowledge and skills working in the fire-rescue and EMS fields.

Chapter 4

May I Have Some Cheese With My Wine?

WHILE ON PATROL late one evening, my partner and I came upon a car on the highway that was driving erratically. The vehicle would drift off the right shoulder, back into the right lane, across the centerline and back into it's lane of travel. We followed for a short distance. My partner turned on the emergency lights and sounded the siren to get the attention of the driver. Once the sedan came to a stop, we exited our vehicle and approached the car with our flashlights. My partner began to converse with the male driver. I shined my flashlight around the interior. I observed a bottle of wine lying on the seat between the two. As I continued to visually sweep the interior, I saw that the female was holding a water glass against the passenger door with her foot. I noted the water glass contained a dark blue substance. I tapped on the window and asked the female to open the door so that I might examine the contents of the glass.

She replied, "What glass?"

I said, "The glass you're holding against the door's interior." I stepped to the side so she could open her door.

As she opened her door, I bent forward to take hold of the water glass. She grabbed it and in a swift motion flung the contents into my face. She then stated, "Well, there goes your evidence!"

I reached across the seat, withdrew a half-full wine bottle and said, "This will do just fine."

The wine ran down my face, uniform shirt and protective ballistic vest. I was soaked. My partner watched in disbelief from across the roofline. I instructed the female to step out of the vehicle, follow me to the rear of the car and take a seat on the trunk. I redirected my attention to my partner who had removed the driver and had him step in front of our cruiser. My partner explained that he would perform a field sobriety test. The female began shouting obscenities and calling us pigs and oinkers. I told her to remain quiet, but that only resulted in further obscenities. My partner completed the field sobriety tests, which the driver failed miserably, then told him that he was being placed under arrest for driving while intoxicated. He told him to turn and face the patrol unit. The driver told us that his home was less than a quarter of a mile away and indicated that we could see his front-porch light from our location. He asked us to allow him to go home with the understanding that he would not drive the rest of the night.

My partner told him, "Your girlfriend just poured a glass of wine all over my partner, she has continuously shouted obscenities and been belligerent the entire time we have been conducting our investigation. The time to ask us for a favor has long passed."

My partner had retrieved his handcuffs and was about to put them on the driver when the driver said, "Sir, I will go to jail peacefully with no trouble, but may I please have a word with my girlfriend before we go?" My partner agreed. The driver walked to the rear of his vehicle where his girlfriend sat and said, "Thanks, b---h." He then backhanded her in the face, knocking her off the trunk of the car and into the ditch line.

My partner grabbed and cuffed the driver while I pulled the crying female from the ground. I asked, "Ma'am, would you like to press charges against this man?"

She screamed and cried but declined to press charges. We called for a second unit to transport the female, a wrecker to impound the car and transported the intoxicated driver to jail to be booked for operating under the influence (OUI). He demanded a non-jury trial before a judge on his driving under the influence charge. Under testimony, I explained the erratic manner in which he was driving, inability to complete field sobriety tests, wine being thrown all over my duty uniform by the female, and how belligerent she was the entire time.

The judge asked me if my uniform required dry cleaning after the incident and I answered, "Yes, Your Honor." He asked how much the cleaning cost me and I told him. The judge slapped the gavel and declared a verdict of guilty which included jail time, court costs plus fifteen dollars restitution for the cleaning of my uniform. I thought, *there is such a thing as karma!*

Chapter 5

---∾---

A Double Header

ONE NIGHT WHILE working with the police department, my partner and I intercepted a vehicle being driven erratically. Our traffic stop would result in the driver being placed under arrest for operating under the influence and taken to jail. We processed the driver at the jail and headed back to our jurisdiction. As we made our way, we came to an intersection. We saw a man lying on the edge of the roadway against a guard rail. We activated our lights, got out of the car and walked to the man. He began to pull himself using the guardrail and he said, "Boy, am I happy to see you guys--I almost drowned."

I said, "You nearly drowned?"

He replied, "Yes, my car went into the river and I nearly drowned getting out of the car."

With our flashlights we looked beyond the guardrail and saw the back end of a car in the river below. He had driven down a hill, left the roadway and ended up in the river below, completely mising the guardrail. His speech was slurred; he was unsteady on his feet and smelled of alcohol. We ran field sobriety tests, which he failed. We were out of our jurisdiction and contacted the county sheriff's department for one of their units to come and handle the arrest. The duty sergeant informed us that all their units were tied up on calls and told us that we were being deputized to handle the arrest and to transport the driver back to the jail. We returned and processed our second OUI in less than an hour. A few weeks later, we were at the sheriff's office picking up some paperwork to have processed and visited with the sergeant. The police radio was non-stop traffic, as it was a very busy night across the county.

A call for assistance came in as we stood there. The sergeant threw his hands in the air and said, "I'm out of cars and have no one available to handle this call."

I said, "We'll take the call, Sergeant."

He replied, "You can't go, it's out of your jurisdiction."

I said, "Sure we can. You deputized us two weeks ago."

He chuckled, "That was only to handle the arrest of the intoxicated driver. You are now un-deputized!"

We all laughed and headed back to our area.

Chapter 6

A QUIET SUMMER AFTERNOON

ON A BRIGHT sunny Saturday afternoon, we were patrolling and decided to make a drive-thru at a large campground in the area. The warmth and sunshine had drawn many to enjoy camping, fishing, boating, and picnicking along the shoreline. As we entered the campground we met a state trooper coming out. We pulled our units off the roadway and struck up a conversation. We had worked many times with him; he was very personable and had a great sense of humor. As we conversed, he made a comment about how "quiet" it was around the community. He had no sooner said that, when the dispatch center began to obtain a location check of all the county units. You can tell by the tone in a dispatcher's voice when they are anxious; they speak in a rapid-fire manner. When the location check was complete, she identified two patrol units and provided information of a large fight in progress, involving chains and knives, on the beach across the street from the campgrounds.

I told the trooper, "So much for a quiet afternoon, let's go!"

My partner grabbed the radio, told dispatch that we were a two-man unit across the street from the beach and we also had a trooper right behind us. She acknowledged his radio transmission and told us that additional back-up units were on the way. A quick trip across the highway and into the beach area and we were on the scene. From my driver's seat I saw a large fight involving at least fifteen to eighteen individuals wielding chains, knives, and baseball bats. Several people lay scattered on the ground, bleeding from injuries they had sustained. I ran toward one man curled up, holding his right side. I saw that he had been stabbed and bright frothy blood was coming from a chest wound. I told him to keep pressure over the wound and medical help was on the way. I pulled my radio from my beltline, called the dispatch center, and told them we had multiple injuries. I requested ambulances and additional PD units ASAP! As more and more officers arrived, we were able to get the situation under control. Several people were taken into custody on various charges.

The ambulance service asked me if I could ride in the back to provide care for the stabbing victim. I ran to my partner and told him I would be going to the hospital in an ambulance. He said he would meet me there. I climbed into the back of the rig and headed to the hospital. The patient had suffered a stab wound that had penetrated his lung. I treated the wound, provided 100% oxygen, and monitored his vital signs on the way. We arrived and he was handed off to the hospital staff for continued treatment. I walked out of the treatment room to be met by our county sheriff. He asked me what in the hell had gone on out there. I told him I didn't know the details of the circumstances that precipitated the fight, but it reminded me of a gladiator movie when we got on the scene.

Over a period of fifteen minutes, additional ambulances arrived, bringing in the wounded. Injuries included severe head lacerations, skull fractures, broken arms, jaws, and ribs. The incident brought in police agencies, which included two additional townships, city PD, sheriff's deputies from two counties, as well as several state troopers. An impromptu command post was created for agencies to process information and obtain statements from the victims. Officers remained on the scene to interview witnesses who provided details on what sparked the altercation as well as identify those who used weapons to injure. The event which triggered the fight was when a youngster was knocked to the ground by a large dog which was running loose in the picnic area (dogs are prohibited). The youngster's father exchanged harsh words with the dog's owner, which resulted in hostilities being exchanged between the two. The exchange of words quickly escalated into a physical altercation. Friends and family members rushed to back the combatants. It rapidly turned into total chaos as some ran to their vehicles to retrieve bats and chains. As a result of this event two people were charged and convicted with attempted murder, others were charged with aggravated assault. What had begun as a pleasant day at the lake had erupted in violence, bloodshed, and several people being arrested and hospitalized.

Chapter 7

ALL POINTS BULLETIN

ON A COLD dreary night of a Halloween weekend while working for the police department, an APB (all-points bulletin) came from the dispatch center for a subject wanted in connection with two felonies. This nomenclature has changed over the years and is now referred to as a BOLO (be on the lookout). A name and description of the suspect's vehicle was provided with license plate numbers. A friend of mine had been wanting to do a ride along for sometime. I was able to get permission from the chief, so my friend was riding in the back seat. My partner and I discussed the possibility that this person could be located at a home of a friend a few miles away. We felt it was worthwhile to drive by and take a look. We drove to the home where we thought the individual might be. We approached slowly. As we passed the home, we observed a vehicle matching the description of the vehicle in the alert. I continued to drive past the house and went down the road to an intersection to stop. My partner was on the radio, contacting dispatch to report that we had a match on the suspect's vehicle. We were instructed to stand down and wait for backup to arrive.

About eight to ten minutes had passed when a two-man sheriff's patrol unit slowly rolled in behind us. We all got together to discuss an approach plan, which would be led by the sheriff's deputies. We got back into our units with the deputies taking the lead. We approached the home and the deputies pulled into the yard, coming to a stop beside the parked pickup. I parked our patrol unit about three car lengths behind the deputies. My nerves were quivering as I stepped from the car, my eyes fixed on the pickup in the driveway, which faced the roadway. I rationalized that the truck had been parked in such a position to make a quick getaway. The deputy on the driver's side stepped out of the vehicle and put his uniform hat on, grabbed his flashlight, and closed his door as his partner was exiting the passenger side door.

With light provided from the front porch I saw someone suddenly sit upright in the pickup and saw the barrel of a long gun. I yelled, "In the truck, he has a gun."

My warning was not in time, as the man leapt from the truck, sticking the barrel of the gun into the throat of the deputy. The man was screaming at the deputy, all the while holding the barrel of the gun on the deputy. The deputy held his hands away from his sides with his hands open and clearly visible. I had already drawn my service weapon and taken a position behind the left fender of our cruiser. The deputy and assailant stood between the truck and the sheriff's patrol unit. The second deputy had taken cover behind the right front corner of their unit and was not in a position to fire his weapon, with his partner in direct line of fire. My partner took cover on the right side of our patrol unit.

I waited for an opportunity and screamed at the assailant. He turned his head toward me. I pulled the hammer back on my service revolver and said, "Do not turn your head away from me. Slowly lower the gun, and do it now!"

He was looking directly down the barrel of my firearm. While still looking in my direction, he slowly raised the gun skyward and the deputy grabbed the shotgun from him. The situation ended without shots being fired. The deputies handled the situation from there. I walked back to our cruiser, I holstered my side arm, sweat dripping from my face despite the chilly night temperature. I walked around to the driver's door to see my friend huddled on the floorboard of the back seat. As I got in and removed my uniform hat, my hand shook as I tried to put the key in the ignition.

My ride-along friend pulled himself up to the protective cage between the front and rear seat and said, "You know, Curt, I thought for a few moments someone was going to get killed out there."

I looked into the rearview mirror at him and said, "Yeah, so did I."

Chapter 8

THE HEARTBREAK OF HOPELESSNESS

WHILE MOST OF my work with the police department was relatively uneventful, there were a few times when I was involved in some pretty crazy situations. One such time occurred in the late evening hours of a Saturday night. While on patrol, my partner and I received a radio call from our dispatch requesting our back-up assistance to one of our sheriff's patrol units. We had a great working relationship with our deputies and state troopers and backed each other up anytime the need arose. On this particular evening, we would provide assistance for a report of a man with a gun, who was threatening his family. The location of the incident would require about a twelve-minute response time. We were instructed to meet with two deputies at a specified location and to use a silent approach. I was driving when the call came in, so my partner handled the radio traffic. Most of our travel would be on open paved roadways, but there was a stretch that was quite hilly. I had my foot pressed to the floor as we made our way. We arrived with the deputies in about ten minutes. We slipped in behind the two-man sheriff's patrol unit, and got out of the car.

Using our cars for cover, we discussed a course of action. The home sat on top of a hill with a circular driveway leading to the top. There was a heavily wooded area at the back of the home. Once the plan was laid out by the senior deputy, we slowly drove up the drive to the top of the hill. We positioned our cruisers in opposing directions to provide us temporary cover. I slid from my seat, removing the department's shotgun from its locked rack. My partner took a defensive position behind his door. Receiving a nod from a deputy, I slowly began working my way from tree to tree, advancing toward the front of the home. When I had gotten as close to the home as I could with cover provided, I turned back and nodded to the deputies. With the shotgun trained on the front of the home, both deputies began to slowly advance, with one fanning out to the left side of the home and the other coming up parallel to me, about twenty yards to my right. My partner advanced on my right flank. The first deputy had worked himself into position at the left front corner of the house where he had hoped to obtain visual reconnaissance through a kitchen window. I held my shotgun directed at the front of the home and my eyes sweeping from left to right watching the front windows and the open garage door.

Just as the deputy was reaching the front window, a shot rang out from inside the house. The deputy closest to the front window yelled, "Let's go!" He ran across the front of the house into the garage. I raised the shotgun and followed the deputy. He charged through the garage and with one kick took the interior door completely off its hinges. He swung to the left with his side arm drawn. I was right behind him sweeping to the right, checking for danger. As the deputy stepped into the living room, he looked down and slowly began to holster his side arm. I walked to where he was standing and there was a man lying on the floor with a large-caliber handgun near him. He had taken his own life. The family members had barricaded themselves in a bedroom so the husband could not gain access, then slipped out of the home through the bedroom window and escaped through the woods and were safe.

The telephone in the living room began to ring, I walked to the table were the phone was located, pulled my handkerchief from my pocket, placed it over the phone receiver, and answered it. A man's voice said, "Whom am I speaking with?"

I instantly recognized the voice on the other end as being the duty sergeant at the sheriff's office. He asked me what the situation was. I told him what had occurred and that family members were safe. He said, "Thanks, Curtis. You guys lock the scene down and I'll get detectives on the way to process it."

As I stood there, I wondered, *what kind of circumstances would create such a feeling of hopelessness that suicide could be the only answer?*

Chapter 9

———— ❧ ————

THIS IS WHAT WE DO!

MY WIFE AND I were returning home from an afternoon visiting with family. We turned at an intersection leading toward home and entered a sharp left curve. As we came out of the curve, I saw a passenger car flipping end over end. Through the dust created by the tumbling car, I saw multiple bodies flying through the air. I quickly pulled off the roadway onto the berm and put on my hazard lights. I grabbed my portable radio and ran toward the first victim while simultaneously calling the dispatch center with information and location. I told them there was a vehicle crash with four ejections. I requested two advanced life support units and two basic life support units to my location. I systematically went from one victim to the next, performing a rapid assessment of their conditions. When I had performed a triage of the four victims, I got on my radio and requested a helicopter to be sent to the hospital. The dispatcher asked which air service I wanted. I told her the closest available.

A young man covered in dirt walked up to me and asked me if I had a cigarette. I asked, "Were you in this car?"

He answered in a casual manner, "Yeah, I was driving." He had been thrown from his tumbling vehicle and had not even received as much as a scratch. He smelled of alcohol and had been driving too rapidly to negotiate the sharp curve in the road.

As circumstances would have it, two of my EMS colleagues had just dropped a patient at the hospital. Upon hearing my radio traffic, one said to his partner, "I think Curt has some serious shit going down. We had better get out there!" As the local fire department arrived, I began directing their personnel to the victims based on my physical findings, priority one, priority two, and priority three, based on the extent and seriousness of injuries. Multiple ambulances arrived within a short time to assist the fire department rescue members in the treating and loading of patients. I heard the chop of the inbound helicopter in the distance as we continued to work. One of our paramedics requested a second helicopter to be activated and dispatched to the hospital. When the last of the patients had been loaded and transported, I got back in the car with my wife. I made my way slowly through the number of emergency vehicles that had responded to the scene and headed home. Our drive would take us past the local hospital, where one helicopter was already on the landing pad. The second chopper approached and landed in an open grassy area across the street from the hospital. It would have been completely understandable for those who passed by in the middle of this mayhem to expect that there would be fatalities involved. Miraculously, all five occupants recovered from their injuries. Had these young people been wearing their seat belts, they very likely would have remained inside the car and not sustained the injuries they received. My wife worked as a nurse in a hospital or doctor's office her entire career and had never been on the scene of a vehicle crash. This was an eye-opening experience to her, regarding how we work in the pre-hospital setting. She told me later that she was very impressed by how everyone worked together.

I said, "This is what we do!"

Chapter 10

IT'S NOT DESTINATION,
IT'S THE JOURNEY

- Ralph Waldo Emerson

I'VE ALWAYS HAD a love of motorcycles and have owned several during my lifetime. I enjoyed the freedom of riding with the wind in my face. It was therapeutic and relaxing when I felt stressed. On occasion, my wife would accompany me. Although not an avid rider, she would enjoy an occasional ride through the countryside. She is what I call a fair-weather rider. The weather conditions had to be near perfect with temperatures in the range of 70-80, and sunshine. My parents never understood why I would ride a motorcycle, considering the number of times I've had to respond and deal with the aftermath of multiple crashes involving motorbikes. I told them I recognized the hazards involved but my experiences made me a very cautious rider.

One day, with the weather conditions meeting my wife's expectations, we climbed on my Harley and headed out for an afternoon of riding. We had traveled several miles on a paved county road when I saw a cloud of dust three to four hundred feet in front of us. Within the dust cloud, I saw a car tumbling off the road and into an embankment. I called out to my wife that there had been an accident and I would be stopping to check for injuries. I rolled slightly past the overturned SUV and threw the kick stand down, pulled my helmet off and placed it on the rearview mirror. Still dressed in leather chaps and jacket, I walked toward the vehicle. Observing the SUV had sheared off a utility pole, I checked for a downed powerline. The pole had been sheared but remained upright, supporting all lines. The SUV had ended upside down in the embankment with the driver inside lying on his back. I wiggled inside through the shattered side window to perform a patient assessment. First, I checked the ABC's in lay terms, making sure that he had a good airway, his breathing was adequate, and he had circulation of blood through his system.

I had just finished when a man began yelling at me outside the car. I turned toward him and I rather briskly yelled, "What?"

He said, "My wife is a nurse and she is standing back there." He pointed behind the accident scene.

I said, "Great, my wife is a nurse too! Have your wife go visit with my wife standing beside the Harley."

I returned my attention to the unconscious driver and continued to perform an assessment for broken bones. Suddenly, someone grabbed me by my riding boots and jerked me feet first from inside of the car. The sudden extraction caused my chin to bounce off the door frame. Angrily I spun around. I was looking into the face of one of our sheriff's deputies.

He instantly recognized me and said, "Oh shit, Curtis! I didn't know it was you. Get back in there."

He would later apologize and tell me he thought that some biker had stumbled into the scene and decided to see what was going on. Within a few moments, the local fire department arrived and I assisted them in immobilizing the patient for removal from the vehicle. When we were ready to remove him, I heard the sound of a helicopter overhead. The aircraft landed behind my motorcycle in an open field. My wife had a front row seat for the excitement. We carried the driver to the medical helicopter, and within moments he was whisked away to the trauma center.

Chapter 11

TIME FOR A SWIM

A 911 CALL was sent out reporting a car that had gone off the roadway and into a river not far from the fire department. I responded and was the first to arrive on the scene. I could see the car bobbing in the river. The roofline was barely visible as the current carried it away from me. I ran to the riverbank, pulling off my shoes and shirt as I made my way through the brush to the riverbank. I peeled off my slacks, dove into the water, and swam to the area where I had last seen the vehicle. I dove down, located the submerged car and pulled on the passenger door handle attempting to open it. Unfortunately, the car had settled into the silt on the river bottom and the door would not open. In the murky water, the visibility was nearly zero. I felt along the top of the window and found that the window was partially rolled down. I placed my knees against the door, grabbed the top edge of the glass, and pulled. The glass shattered. I reached into the vehicle, performing arm sweeps, attempting to find anyone inside. I returned to the surface for a breath of air and dove to make a second sweep, then swam to the driver's side and repeated the same sequence, only to discover that there was no one inside. When I surfaced, the local fire chief and a state trooper had arrived and were standing on the river bank.

I yelled to them that I had performed sweeps of the car and found no one in it. I began swimming toward the shore when I heard the dispatch center ask the fire chief if he would like the sheriff's department dive team activated.

He replied, "Negative, we have a diver in the water."

I thought, *Well, he didn't lie to the dispatcher; I am a diver;* However, I had no dive equipment with me and I was swimming in my underwear. As I approached the river bank, the trooper called out, "Hey, since you're already in the water, would you mind going back down and get the license plate number for me?"

I said, "Sure, I can do that." I turned and swam back to the area of the submerged vehicle. I dove, swam to the back of the car and placed my face nearly against the license plate to read the numbers due to the extremely murky conditions. I rose to the surface and called out the plate number to the trooper. I made my way to shore where my clothes were lying in the grass. A young female EMT standing beside the fire chief began to giggle. The chief admonished her and told her to get back to the ambulance and get me some towels for me to use.

The chief said, "You're bleeding." He took hold of my left hand, and only then did I realize I had a gash across the palm. The chief called back to the ambulance and instructed them to bring first aid supplies back to treat my hand. As my hand was being disinfected and bandaged, others were wiping my back and shoulders with towels. I slipped back into my dry clothes as the trooper came walking back from his cruiser. He informed us that the vehicle in the water had been stolen from its owner during the previous night. The thief had probably ditched the car in the river. Little did I know that my hand laceration was not the only thing I received from my failed rescue attempt. Within an hour of leaving the river, my legs, abdomen and chest began to itch. It soon became clear that I must have ran through a patch of poison ivy in my haste to get to the submerged vehicle. I got home, took a shower, and covered myself in copious amounts of calamine lotion. The next day I went to the doctor's office and received a steroid injection and a prescription for prednisone pills. After a period of absolute misery, the medication took hold and relieved the intense inching.

Chapter 12

DINNER WILL HAVE TO WAIT

ONE SUMMER EVENING, my wife and I made plans to go to dinner with some good friends. As we were driving and conversing, my wife was telling our friends that she had never seen an automobile accident happen before she married me. However, since we'd been together, she had seen two and watched me work the scene of both. No sooner had she gotten those words out than I saw a flash of headlights in front of us, glass flying in the air, and cars swerving in front of our vehicle. Our friend, who was driving, stopped the car. I jumped out and told them to call 911 and get help coming. I ran to the car which had been struck head on by a large pickup. I found a young woman slumped over in driver's seat. She was pinned against the steering wheel by an entire load of household goods that had been thrust forward by the sudden impact.

I recognized that she could not breathe adequately, so I

ran to the back of the station wagon, jerked the tailgate open, and began throwing everything onto the highway. Other good Samaritans came to the back and asked what they could do to help. I yelled, "She's suffocating! Get everything out!"

With the additional help, we emptied the rear of the car. I positioned myself behind the young mother and gently raised her head while applying slight upward pressure on her head and neck. I spoke softly to her, asked where she was in pain and kept her calm until an EMS unit arrived.

The medics came up to the driver's side window and one said, "What you got, Curt?" I looked up to see two of my colleagues standing there. I provided them information that I had acquired and continued to maintain cervical spine traction until the fire department had removed the driver's door. My colleagues applied a cervical immobilizing device and half back board. She had sustained internal injuries as she was forcefully thrown into the steering wheel. My EMS friends transported her to a local hospital just a few minutes away. I walked back to the car where my wife and friends were waiting. They asked me about her injuries.

My friend said, "You know, Curt, I don't think it's a coincidence that these accidents happen in front of you. I think God places you in a position of being there to help those people."

Chapter 13

───────❧❧───────

WHAT DO YOU THINK MY CHANCES ARE?

ONE DAY AT the fire station, we received a call for a vehicle accident on a state roadway not far away. During our drive, we received additional information that there were minor injuries at the scene and we could slow our response to normal traffic. We arrived at an intersection to find that a car had struck a stopped vehicle that was waiting for traffic to clear before making a left-hand turn. I approached the driver of the vehicle that had struck the stopped car. He was a frail elderly gentleman in his nineties.

I asked him where he was hurt. He said, "Well, I bounced my face on the steering wheel, but other than that, I'm fine."

I examined his forehead and he had received a small bruise and a bloody nose. As I spoke with him, a deputy sheriff pulled up and approached. He asked me how the driver was and I told him that he was okay.

The deputy said, "I'll be right back," and walked to the driver of the vehicle he had struck. The deputy returned and asked the elderly man to provide him with his driver's license, proof of insurance, and vehicle registration. The man began searching through the glove compartment and arm rest for the necessary documents. He slowly sifted through a pile of papers over a period of several minutes and was able to locate the proof of insurance and registration. He handed them to the deputy standing beside me.

The deputy stated again, "Sir, I need your driver's license."

"Oh yes," the man said, reaching for his wallet. He sorted through his wallet and slowly handed it to the deputy. The deputy thanked him and told him he would be back in a few moments.

I watched as the deputy walked towards his cruiser examining the license he had just been handed. Halfway to his car the deputy stopped, turned around, and walked back to the car where I was standing.

He said, "Sir! Do you have another driver's license on you?"

The gentleman replied, "They only give you one of those."

The deputy said, "I understand that but your license expired several years ago."

The officer was holding the driver's license in his right hand while his left hand rested on the windowsill of the driver's door. The deputy said, "Sir! You can't be driving with an expired operator's license. You must go to the department of motor vehicles and get a new license."

The elderly man reached out and lightly patted the deputy

on the back of his hand and said, "Son, what do you think my chances are?"

The deputy stated, "Sir, I don't know, but you can't be driving without a valid license."

I felt sorry for the elderly man because he knew he wouldn't be able to pass the tests necessary to obtain a new license and he would have to give up driving. I felt badly because I realized that we all may face that situation one day. The deputy issued citations for failure to stop in clear distance and operating a vehicle with an expired operator's license.

Chapter 14

NOT ALL WOUNDS ARE VISIBLE

A 911 CALL was received by our dispatch center for a report of a man threatening to commit suicide who had barricaded himself in the bathroom. We responded from the fire station but were given instructions not to approach until we had police officers on the scene. We staged up about a block from the residence and waited for deputies to arrive. Within minutes, a patrol unit pulled in and we waited for further instructions. My impatience got the best of me. I instructed my driver to pull up near the front entrance. I told my crew that I was going to the front door to obtain a situational update. Stepping into the doorway, I was met by one of the deputies who told me that the man had a double-edged razor blade with him in the bathroom. They had confirmed with others in the home that no other weapons were available to him. I stepped into the hallway where the second deputy was standing watch over the door. The deputies were trying to figure out how to handle the situation. I suggested that we remove a heavy blanket from the bedroom; I would stand with the blanket in front of me and one of them would kick the door in and I would throw the blanket over the man's head. The man's natural instinct would be to throw his hands in the air to catch the blanket. I would rush through the doorway protected in my firefighter gear. The deputies would then follow me in to restrain and secure him.

They agreed with my suggested plan of action. I pulled my Nomex hood in place, secured the heavy collar around my neck and lowered the visor of my helmet in front of my face. A deputy had already obtained a blanket from a nearby bedroom. I took the blanket and folded the top half which would unfurl as it went toward the man. When I gave a nod to the deputy, he leaned with his back against the back wall of the hallway and slammed his foot against the door. As the door flew open, I charged through the door throwing the blanket over the head of the man and tackled him. My momentum took both him and me into the bathtub with both deputies fighting for control of his hands through the blanket that enveloped both of us.

A deputy grabbed my wrist in the struggle and I called out, "Wrong arm!"

The man was secured and taken by ambulance for evaluation. When he saw the blanket coming at his head level, he had thrown his hands up, releasing the razor blade and it had fallen harmlessly to the floor. As we would learn, this man was suffering from psychiatric issues. Two years later we received a dispatch and responded to a residence for a report of a stabbing victim. Again, we were instructed not to approach until the scene was secured. When we got in the vicinity of the address, I recognized the home as being the same as the previous incident. We contacted dispatch that we were staged in the area. As we waited, a hysterical female came from the front of the house yelling that her son was unconscious and bleeding and needed immediate help. I told my team to stay put and I would take a closer look. I cautiously approached the front of the home, poked my head inside the living room and there was a man lying on the sofa with the handle of a butcher knife sticking out of his chest.

The blade was pulsating left to right like a metronome keeping time. I recognized that the movement of the knife handle was in sync with his heartbeat. I surmised that the blade had either penetrated the heart or the aorta. I asked, "Who did this?"

The lady of the house said, "He did."

He had placed the butcher knife on a tabletop and thrown himself onto the knife. Once I knew it was self-inflicted, I called my rescue team members on my portable radio to move in. I switched channels, contacted our inbound ambulance, and provided the details of the injury along with a set of vitals. I recommended that he be flown to a trauma center due to the knife impalement.

There was a potential of further harm by movement and the bouncing of a ground ambulance. My paramedic colleagues agreed with my call and ordered a helicopter be flown to our location. The handle of the knife was immobilized by stacking sterile cloths around it and then taping it into place. The ambulance crew arrived and started two IV lines. One hundred percent oxygen was already being given at the time they arrived. I walked across the street, sized up the neighbor's front yard and found it to be satisfactory for a helicopter landing zone.

A voice from behind me said, "May I ask what you're doing?" I replied, "I'm sorry, sir, I'm going to need to use your front yard to land a helicopter." He asked me if it would cause any damage and I assured him it would not. Within five minutes the chopper was in sight. The pilot contacted me via radio and I provided the flight team a patient update and that the landing zone was secured for their touch down.

The patient was loaded in the ground ambulance and rolled very slowly across the street to the landing zone and hand carried to the awaiting helicopter for a flight to a level one trauma center. Later we learned that the knife blade in his chest was lying right next to the aorta, the largest blood vessel in the body. Surgeons were successful in removing the impaled knife from his chest and he fully recovered from his wound. I never knew if this man received the psychiatric help he so desperately needed.

Chapter 15

We Happened To Be In The Neighborhood

I WAS ON transport delivering a man to a local hospital. After we completed the run and filed our report, we prepped the unit for service and left the hospital. It was nearly two o'clock in the morning and I asked my crew if anyone wanted a cup of coffee. The answer was a unanimous yes! We stopped at a convenience store just around the corner from the hospital and each got a coffee to go. There have been a few times in my career that I get some kind of feeling that something isn't right. It is a feeling of anxiousness and impending doom; my stomach tightens and the hair on my neck stands up. This was one of those times. I told my crew, "I have a bad feeling." One member said, "Like what?" I said, "I'm not sure."

We climbed aboard our unit to begin our trip back to the

fire station. As we made our way, a call went out to a neighboring department for a report of an unknown accident. The term "unknown accident" was given when no details of an incident were available. The term "injury accident" was provided if information was available to the dispatch center that there were confirmed injuries reported. The term "property damage" indicated there were no injuries but vehicle damage did occur. Back in my day with the police department, ten-codes were used to designate an injury accident versus a property damage incident. A vehicle damage collision was dispatched as a 10- 37, a collision with injuries, 10-38 and could be given a prefix of a number one, two, or a three with a 138, meaning minor injuries, 238 more serious injuries, and 338, meaning life-threatening injuries were likely. Much has changed over the years. Now most ten codes are no longer used. The reason for this is, under the national response plan (NRP), if an agency should go from one jurisdiction to another, such as the other side of their state or get called upon to perform disaster operations in another state those areas may use different codes and this would create serious communication problems.

Our neighboring department answered their call and were given the location of the unknown accident. When the dispatcher provided the coordinates of this incident, I realized that we were very close to the scene. I got on the radio and provided our neighboring department our location and asked if they would like us to head that way to provide assistance. They replied in the affirmative and requested that we provide them an update when we arrived. I acknowledged, activated our emergency equipment and continued to the dispatch location. We turned off the paved highway onto a gravel road to the scene. My driver started down a steep hill, when in the darkness we observed man waving a flashlight.

We stopped, I climbed from my officer's seat and approached the gentleman standing in the roadway. I said, "Sir, is there an accident here?" I did not see anything except his car parked in the roadway with its hazard flashers activated. He did not verbally respond to my question but instead nodded his head in the affirmative. The man was completely white, absent of any color in his face and appeared to be in a state of shock.

I asked, "Sir, where is the accident?"

Again, a nonverbal response; he pointed with his flashlight off the roadway and down a steep ravine. I walked to the edge of the roadway and I saw a car that had ended up in a wooded area. I rushed down the embankment with flashlight in hand, going through a briar patch that ripped at my hands and face. When I got to the car, there were three victims who all appeared to be in their teens. I checked for signs of life and determined that all three were deceased. As I slowly climbed back up the embankment, I got on the radio and contacted the responding agency to slow their response to normal traffic. I called dispatch to advise them we needed a crash investigator as there were three fatalities at our scene.

The dispatcher replied, "Did you say three fatalities?"

I said, "Affirmative, please start an accident investigator our way."

When our neighboring department arrived, the chief climbed from his engine looked at me and said, "Three, Curtis?"

I replied, "I'm afraid so, Chief."

We awaited the arrival of a deputy sheriff who had the responsibility of investigating the crash site. I went back down with him as he began surveying the scene. He asked, "Do you know any of these young people?"

I said, "I haven't really taken a good look at this point."

I walked around the car. With the aid of my flashlight I gazed into the face of a young lady and my heart sank. I turned away slowly and he said, "You know her, right?"

"Yes," I replied, my voice cracking. There is always a potential of coming across someone you know, or even a family member when working emergency services in your community. This was one of those times. For well over an hour I assisted the deputy, by holding his measuring tape and his flashlight while he the took photographs of the scene. The deputy took pictures from various angles capuring the vehicle as it was in the woods. By the time he had completed his investigation, the sun was coming up and we began the process of removing the bodies for transport to the morgue. After being up all night, I finally made it home for a shower and some rest. My wife awoke and asked me where I had been all night. I told her about the accident that claimed the lives of three high school students.

The sudden loss of their classmates and friends sent the school and community into a state shock and disbelief. The deputy has since retired and we happened to cross paths at a local restaurant one evening. We greeted each other and introduced our spouses. We visited for a short time when the deputy said, "You know, Curt, we've seen a lot of shit together over the years, haven't we?"

I said, "Yes, we've seen more than our fair share."

My wife is amazed by the number of times we have been

driving and a particular site will bring a flashback about an incident I was involved with at some point in my career. I can remember incidents that occurred thirty years ago in great detail, and I doubt those memories will ever fade.

Chapter 16

SCREAMS IN THE DARKNESS

MY FAMILY AND I spent a nice afternoon with some friends at their lake home on a beautiful summer afternoon. We enjoyed a barbeque, our children played in the lake, and we enjoyed our day together. When it got dark my wife took the children home to get them ready for bed. My friend and I sat at his kitchen table enjoying a glass of iced tea and a pleasant conversation. It was beautiful evening and a slight breeze blowing through the dining room window was very comfortable. As we chatted, we heard the screech of car tires on the road in front of his home. We both spun our heads toward the open window as we heard a sickening thud and saw something fly through the air. We bolted for the door and ran out into the roadway. A neighbor's child had been struck by a car and was lying in the middle of the roadway. I began to do an assessment on the youngster and told my friend, who was also on the department, to get his truck and block the roadway with his emergency lights on.

As I worked, I heard blood-curdling screams coming from over my shoulder. The driver of the car had no idea she had struck a child and was screaming hysterically. Moments later, a second woman began screaming. The boy's mother had heard the commotion and ran outside to find her seriously injured child lying in the street. Both the driver and the mother's screams were ear-piercing as I continued to work on the little one. I heard the sirens of our department's rescue in the distance. I got on the radio and provided information about the patient and equipment I wanted as soon as they arrived.

Moments later they were on the scene. We worked to secure a cervical collar and place the youngster on a backboard. We started him on oxygen and obtained a set of vital signs. Our members tried to calm the hysterical driver and mother. We placed the youngster in the back of the rescue. Once inside, we continued to reassess, now that we had good light to better visualize the young boy. He began to convulse violently, which made us extremely concerned about a serious head injury. We made a decision to call a medical helicopter for transport to the trauma center. We drove to a large parking lot about a mile from the incident site and continued to monitor him until the flight team arrived. They climbed into the back of our unit; we provided the team our findings and vitals we had captured while he was under our care. We assisted in loading him into the helicopter which was still running with the pilot inside. When they closed the doors, the turbine screamed to life and they were airborne and off into the night sky. The youngster would spend several days in the intensive care unit but would eventually recover from his injuries. Any first responder would tell you, if they are honest, that the calls involving children are the most difficult to deal with. All through this event I had worked doing exactly as I was taught and trained to do, but when it was over, I was emotionally drained. Sleep was scarce that night as I replayed the event over and over. I could not get the sounds of screaming out of my head.

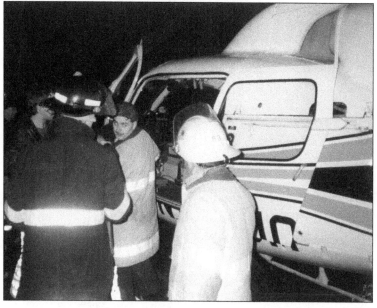

Printed with permission of Michigan Medicine

Chapter 17

ENVIRONMENTAL
NIGHTMARE AVERTED

A STATE HIGHWAY in our district is a major truck route. The trucks carry everything from lumber, chemicals, gasoline, farm machinery, and heavy equipment to home goods and groceries. Once we had a load of whiskey overturned, which drew the attendance from the BATF (Bureau of Alcohol, Tobacco and Firearms). On this particular day we received a call for an overturned box truck on one of the curves in the highway. We loaded up and responded with a rescue crew followed by an engine crew. My engineer rolled up and I had him stop a considerable distance from the crash until I could determine what was being carried. The truck driver was uninjured, so I motioned for him to come back to speak to me. He told me that his load consisted of ten large stainless-steel containers containing automotive paint. I could see the paint running out of the collapsed side of the trailer and into a small ditch line which followed the edge of the roadway.

The area in which the crash occurred is at the public boat launch site of one our area's many lakes. This particular lake was one of a chain of several lakes that could be easily navigated by small watercraft. The flow of paint was running in the direction of a small culvert which ran under a driveway. I quickly realized that we needed to contain the paint, preventing it from running across the roadway to the lake below. I gave instructions to get a plastic tarp from the fire engine and place it in front of the culvert, then shovel sand and dirt to hold the tarp in place. I placed a call to the dispatch center and requested the state highway department provide a dump truck load of sand to be brought to our location.

Due to our emergency equipment occupying the westbound lane of the highway, traffic was alternately being moved using only the eastbound lane. As a result of the crash, traffic was backing up in both directions. The paint continued to flow, filling the small ditch line. A state trooper arrived on the scene, whom I'd had many opportunities to work with. As the trooper approached me, I saw the amber flashers of a highway truck stuck in traffic about a quarter mile from where we stood. I asked the trooper if she could go get the highway truck out of traffic and up here to the crash site.

"Of course," she replied.

Within a few minutes, the trooper had led the truck to my location. I jumped up on the sideboard of the truck and told the driver where I needed the sand offloaded. The driver emphatically told me that his load was not going to be offloaded.

The state trooper had walked up and was standing beside the truck now, listening to the conversation.

I said, "Listen, we have to use your sand to prevent a load of paint from getting into the lake." He said he was not about to dump his load unless it was approved by his superior. Evidently, my request had not been received by the driver. I said, "Look, I've put in a request for a load of sand to be brought here, and I want it dumped now." He refused. I turned to the trooper and said, "I want that sand offloaded right now or I want this driver arrested for obstruction of an emergency."

The driver said, "You can't do that!"

The trooper responded, "He can't, but I can. Now what's it going to be?"

The driver said, "Alright, where do you want it?"

The driver backed up and dumped the sand which our department members shoveled to create a containment reservoir with tarps and sand. I had placed a request to the dispatch center to contact the USEPA (United States Environmental Protection Agency). A representative from the EPA appeared a little over an hour later and came to where I was standing. He looked at how we had dammed up the culvert and kept the paint from getting over the roadway and said, "Wow! Great job, guys." He told me he would get on the phone and get cleanup equipment coming to mitigate the scene. We would spend the rest of the day and into the evening on site while cleanup efforts were underway. The EPA brought in large vacuum trucks to suck up the huge pool of paint. A large excavator was used to remove the contaminated soil and place it in a lined open top semi-trailer. We assisted in blocking the highway while two large wreckers worked to upright the overturned semi-trailer and remove it from the scene. I have always appreciated the cooperation and assistance from our deputies and state troopers.

Chapter 18

FIRE INVESTIGATION - GOING SOLO

DURING MY YEARS in the fire service, I grasped every opportunity to expand my knowledge by taking classes and training programs. I had completed two classes, a 40 and an 80 hour program in fire investigation. I had the chance to work with an expert in the field from the Michigan State Police. I would walk alongside him and observe as he would meticulously go through a fire scene. He always took time to answer any questions I had. I gained a lot of knowledge from just tagging along with him. One Sunday evening, while relaxing at home, the department received a call for a working structure fire located at a scouting camp along the shoreline of a lake not far from the fire station. I drove to the station and our members were already arriving and jumping into their protective bunker gear. We loaded up the trucks and away we went.

As we made our way to the scene, an orange glow was visible in the skyline. We arrived to find a large camp structure fully engulfed in flames. We pulled hoses from the trucks and sprayed water on the building which was rapidly being consumed. Because of dangerous conditions, we could only fight the fire from the building's exterior. The fire had taken its toll on the structure. The roof caved in, further complicating our efforts to extinguish the flames. Eventually we knocked the fire down and then the process of overhauling began. The term overhaul is used to define the process of separating sections of the structure and digging into the remains to extinguish hidden hot spots to prevent a flare-up.

Fortunately, the camp was not occupied at the time. As our members were completing the process, I began to do a walk-around of the building. I approached the back of the building and found the rear door lying on the ground, partially burned. As I lifted the door and looked at the exterior side, I saw distinct striations on the doorknob. Marks like those are indicative of a tool, such as a pipe wrench or channel locks, being used to twist and forcibly break the lock to enter a building. I stood in the rear doorway and with the aid of a flashlight I scanned the interior of the building. I saw something in the rubble that struck me as very odd. It was a portable fire extinguisher standing upright in the middle of the floor.

My thought was, *how in the world could the building have collapsed, yet the fire extinguisher stood upright in the middle of the ruins?* I made my way to the extinguisher and closely examined it. The safety pin had been removed and the plunger had been depressed, which meant that someone had emptied the firefighting agent. I began to pull the debris of the building away from the area of the extinguisher. As I cleared the concrete floor, I found the extinguisher had been discharged on the floor. I surmised that someone had emptied it so that it could not be used to extinguish the fire. I went to my chief and reported my observations and told him that the fire was an act of arson. He placed a radio call to our dispatch center and requested the assistance of the state police fire investigator. I figured that this would be another great opportunity to work with one of my former instructors.

I assisted my colleagues in cleaning equipment, rolling the many lengths of fire hose, gathering hand tools and loading them back on the trucks. The dispatch center informed my chief that the state police fire investigator was not available; he was in the northern part of the state at an annual conference and would not be available until the end of the week. I told the chief that we needed to take photographs and collect evidence immediately and it couldn't wait until the end of the week; the evidence could be destroyed. Also, whoever started the fire could come back and remove evidence from the scene.

"Are you willing to stay here and do this alone?" he asked.

I replied, "Yes, I'll stay here as long as it takes to try to catch the person that burned this building down."

He left me one of the guys and our pickup truck and he returned to the station to get our equipment cleaned and readied for service. I had assembled very basic evidence collection components consisting of grocery bags, an assortment of plastic bags in varying sizes, adhesive labels, marking pens, mason jars with lids, paint cans, lids, and a very nice 35mm camera equipped with auto-winder and flash attachment and several rolls of film. My evidence kit was at the station and the chief had one of our guys bring it to the scene.

I began by photographing the doorknob at the rear of the building; then I removed it and placed it in a paper shopping bag. I walked into the building and took pictures of the fire extinguisher and the firefighting agent that covered the concrete floor. As I walked through the structure, I saw that several kitchen drawers had been pulled open. It appeared that the drawers had been ransacked and most of their contents removed. I found a few pieces of silverware lying on the floor and took pictures. The building itself had served as the camp kitchen and dining hall. It was approximately thirty-five feet wide by fifty feet long and had a beautiful fieldstone fireplace which stood along the back wall. I walked around the exterior and captured pictures of the structure from all angles. Confident I had captured everything from the interior as well as the exterior in photographs, I began to widen my investigation. On the back side of the building, where the door was located, there was a lawn area. At the back of the lawn there was a fence line which ran along the edge of a wooded area. I walked toward the fence line, shining my flashlight. I could see a small section of fencing was sagging, indicating it had been used as a crossing point.

I walked to that area and shined my light beyond the fence, sweeping its beam from side to side. A path had been worn from the fence trailing off into the woods. Just beyond the fence, I saw a dozen butcher knives buried in the dirt with their long blades reflecting brightly in the beam of my flashlight. I was angered to think that someone would intentionally cause harm or death to someone who could fall and impale themselves on those knives in the darkness. The knives had been placed in the path to prevent anyone from following their escape route. Beyond the knives, the walking path led down a steep hill to the lakeshore below. I theorized that someone had broken into the dining hall, stolen whatever there was of value, emptied the fire extinguisher and then set the building on fire to cover-up the break-in, planted the knives in the walking path and escaped down the hill to an awaiting watercraft.

I took several pictures of the butcher knife blades protruding out of the ground across the walking trail. I used a small gardening hand tool to dig up each one, being careful not to touch the blade with my gloved hand. Holding the blades in the light of my flashlight I could see distinct fingerprints on the blades. Each knife was numbered, placed in a plastic bag and sealed. When that was done, I took them to our truck, along with the fire extinguisher and doorknob. It was nearly dawn when I arrived back at the fire station. I locked up everything I had collected and headed home for a hot shower and some sleep.

I delivered my rolls of film to be developed later that day and created a sketch of the layout of the building, fence line, and location where the doorknob, extinguisher and knives were located. On Friday of that week I received a phone call from the detective with the state police. He asked me about the fire and the value of the structure which was lost. I told him I had collected several pieces of evidence and photographs from the scene. He asked me if I would be available to meet with him the following morning at the station and I assured him I would.

The next morning, he and I went into the training room and sat down over a cup of coffee and I explained what I had found, beginning with the door knob and fire extinguisher. I showed him my pictures that I already had developed. When I flipped to the pictures showing the butcher knife blades sticking out of the ground in the walking trail, he took the photograph from my hand. He stared for a moment in silence, looked at me and threw the picture hard against the tabletop.

He exclaimed, "I want the son of a bitch that did this in jail! I haven't seen anything like this since I left Viet Nam!" Those who fought in the Viet Nam conflict knew the Viet Cong used sharpened bamboo sticks, called punji sticks, buried in the ground to impale and wound our military personnel. He asked me how I had retrieved the knives. I assured him that no prints were disturbed during their removal and handling. I showed him my sketch of the building and surrounding area and identified where each piece of evidence was located on the scene sketch.

He told me to get on the phone to the local state police post and have a trooper come to take the evidence to the crime lab for processing. I did so, only to have a trooper who answered tell me that no one was available and if I wanted my evidence transferred to the crime lab, do it myself. I relayed the message to the detective. He got up from the table, snatched the phone from my hand, loudly identified himself and told the trooper on the other end, "You get me a patrol unit to this fire station right now! I don't want to hear any excuses!"

Within fifteen minutes, a state trooper was flying down the street and into the department parking lot. We loaded the evidence into the trunk of the cruiser and off he went to the crime lab. The detective smiled at me and said, "Well, you did everything you could, except identify and cuff the suspect. Let's see if we can help you get this guy."

Nearly two weeks passed before I received a phone call. The

detective informed me that the investigators had interviewed a young man who confessed to the break-in and setting the arson fire at the campgrounds. The defendant also identified two accomplices that took part that night. With a confession and forensic evidence to prove the three were in the building, committed burglary, set the fire and planted the knives along the walking path, all three were arrested and charged for their crimes. It gave me a feeling of satisfaction that my time and loss of sleep were worth the effort.

Evidence collected from the scene

Evidence collected from the scene

Chapter 19

———❧———

MONTHS OF PLANNING TO COVER ALL BASES

DURING MY YEARS in the fire service we trained continualy. These programs would cover such topics as building search and rescue, external and internal fire attack, ventilation tactics, pumper training, driving course, extrication techniques on salvaged cars, ladder safety, ropes and knots, and other subjects. I was fortunate to have worked with one of our area fire chiefs who was very innovative in creating training scenarios. We served on the county medical control board together. We would discuss our respective department training programs from time to time.

One day, this chief approached me and asked me if I would be interested in hosting a large-scale county-wide disaster simulation. I asked him what he had in mind. He told me he had an idea for a water disaster exercise. I was intrigued by the idea, as there had never been a water disaster simulation done in our area. Our conversation took place in the early fall and we agreed to plan the exercise over the winter and hold it in spring of the following year. He and I would meet several times and also conference call to discuss the details of the exercise. To hold an exercise of this magnitude, with so many area agencies involved, required a lot of planning. The details of the exercise were limited to just a few key people to prevent it from becoming common knowledge around the county's fire service.

Once the plans were finalized and a date had been selected, invitations to participate were sent out to all fire and EMS agencies, two area hospitals, sheriff's department marine divisions from two counties, and two medical helicopter services. We began receiving confirmation from many agencies. As the date of the exercise approached, we were excited about the growing list of participants. One full week before the exercise took place, a public service announcement (PSA) was sent out to all area newspapers, radio stations, and dispatch centers of both counties on which the lake was located. The announcement provided the site, date, and time of the disaster drill and a list of all the agencies that would be taking part. The exercise base would be the shoreline of a church campground which had given us permission to use.

The day of the exercise started very early. My planning partner and I met at the camp beach early and began to unload props that would add realism to the scenario. The chief had secured a tail section of an airplane for our use. We filled it with large blocks of Styrofoam to provide buoyancy. Another member of our department, who was also a diver, and I got into our wet suits and carried our air tanks and fins to the edge of the beach. We pulled the aircraft tail section out into the lake. A pontoon came alongside with cement blocks that were attached with rope and dropped into the water. With cement blocks for weight, the aircraft tail stood perfectly upright on the lake. I had acquired two smoke bombs from a friend, who was an officer in the army reserves, as well as an officer with the department of natural resources. The smoke bombs were fastened to each side of the airplane tail section with adhesive tape. My dive partner and I placed a rope and buoys around the entire area in which the exercise would take part. A pontoon, which had been donated for our use, was brought out and flipped upside down. Floatation cushions, insulated coolers, clothing, folding chairs and other miscellaneous items were thrown into the water to create a debris field. Twenty high school students volunteered to serve as our simulated victims for the drill. Two people applied make-up which made the volunteers look like they were really injured. When our victims had been prepared, they were shuttled out to the exercise area by pontoon boats. Each one of our student victims was given a briefing on how they were to act when first responders arrived. Everyone went through a safety check to make certain their life jackets were on and properly secured before they were allowed to enter the water. When all were in position, I swam over to the aircraft tail and pulled the pins on the smoke bombs. The exercise was underway.

At the prescribed time, our 911 center began alerting fire rescue and EMS units. Dispatchers instructed them over the radio that this was an exercise so that there would be no confusion about it being a real-life event. Shortly, various agencies began to arrive along the shoreline. Medical personnel were sent onto the lake to begin extracting and shuttling the mock victims to shore. A triage area was established on the shoreline with each victim evaluated by priority, priority 1 being the highest. Everything within the circumference of the exercise area on the lake was monitored under the careful watch of two marine boats staffed by sheriff's deputies. They also prevented civilian watercraft from getting close to our operational area. My dive partner and I swam around speaking to our student volunteers to ensure their safety and well-being. A medical helicopter arrived and landed on the lawn adjacent to the beach. The triage, treatment, and transport of our simulated victims went well. However, a few of our students, who were the last to be removed, were beginning to feel the effects of exposure to the water temperature.

We all felt that the drill had been a great achievement. It brought together over twenty agencies who took part in a purposeful training activity that had never taken place before. When the drill was complete, we collected all our props and we learned that both county 911 dispatch centers were flooded with calls from hysterical people reporting an aircraft crash on the lake with heavy smoke and screams of people in the water. We shook our heads and thought, *does anyone read a newspaper or listen to the local radio anymore?* Other than the overload of 911 calls the exercise was a very successful training opportunity.

Smoke plumes results in 911 calls during training exercise.
Printed with permission - The Exponent

Chapter 20

———— ∞ ————

A CASE OF THE HEEBIE-JEEBIES

ONE MORNING, AFTER shift change, my partner and I were making our way back to our coverage area, driving through the country roads. It was springtime; the trees were showing new leaves and the grass was turning lush and green. Farmers had begun to till and prepare their fields for planting. As we rode along, I watched as a farmer plowed a furrow across his field. I noticed that the rear tire of his plow was flat and wobbled from side to side on its rim. I asked my partner to stop the rig so I could alert the farmer about his equipment problem. The farmer, whom I knew, saw me as I walked toward him, stopped and idled the motor.

I called to him and said, "Hey, your back tire is flat."

He jumped from the tractor seat and went back to investigate. He mumbled to himself and then said aloud, "Well, I'll walk to the house and bring back another tire to put on." I told him we would be happy to give him a lift to his home, which was about a quarter mile up the road.

He said, "I appreciate your offer, but to be honest, those things (pointing to our ambulance) give me a case of the hee-bie-jeebies." I chuckled and walked back across the field and climbed into the rig.

A few months later, while returning to the fire station, we were dispatched to a report of an aircraft down. We turned our emergency vehicles around and responded to the location. The plane had gone down in a wooded area just off the highway. We arrived on the scene and found two occupants in an Ultralight aircraft. The craft had crashed nose first into the ground. I went over to the wreckage and checked for vital signs of the occupants. I determined that both had perished on impact. Deputy sheriffs arrived on the scene, along with a command member. The captain asked me if I would be so kind to see if they were carrying identification, so I walked to the wreckage and retrieved the wallets. A deputy opened and removed the driver licenses; he asked me if I knew either of the two. I stared at the picture of the first license and my heart sank. I recognized the man as a prominent member of the community, a local farmer. I provided him directions to where his farm was located. It was the same man who months earlier I had spoken to about his flat tire. When you live and work in a small community, these kinds of heartbreaking scenes do occur.

Chapter 21

CRASH LANDING

ON A BRIGHT and sunny, summer day, while providing coverage at Michigan International Speedway, we received a report of an aircraft that had gone down in a swampy area just north of a state highway near the racetrack. I was in the passenger seat of the department pickup truck which was equiped with a water tank, pump and small diameter hose lines designed to fight wildland fires. I was dressed in my class two dress uniform, which consisted of dark navy-blue dress slacks, white uniform shirt with department insignia on the sleeves, collar pins, name plate, and department badge. My driver turned on the emergency warning equipment as I got on the radio to acknowledge the call for assistance. Since we were very close to the crash site, we arrived in the area in about three minutes. As we were making our way, I saw a TV news helicopter hovering overhead. A passenger in the right seat was pointing toward the ground beneath the chopper. I raised my hand and gave a thumbs up to acknowledge him. We had driven through cattails higher than the roofline of the truck to get close to the crash site. As I made my way into the swamp, my dress shoes were being sucked into the muck, which forced me to grab anything within reach to stay upright. I was on the radio providing directions to the site and I instructed our responding engine crew and rescue that I wanted a foam line pulled in from the engine. The odor of aviation fuel was strong and I knew that it could ignite at any time.

I plodded my way around the fuselage and peeked inside. I could see that there were three occupants and the pilot inside. I told them that additional help was on the way and we would get them out. They all were conscious and injured to varying degrees. The pilot seemed to be the most seriously injured. Due to the condition of the crashed aircraft, I called for the jaws of life to be bought forward from the fire engine. The jaws of life are a set of hydraulic tools used to cut and pry vehicles apart that have been involved in collisions. Our personnel arrived, pulled a hose line in and began covering the area with a thick layer of foam to reduce the potential for a fuel fire. While the foam was being applied, a team was making ready the extrication tools. When I was confident that we had covered the spilled fuel and aircraft adequately, the extrication team began to cut away the roofline of the fuselage and roll it back, providing open access to those trapped inside.

Our trauma bags had been carried in, so work began to assess those inside and a slow deliberate process of treating, back boarding, and removing each one from the wreckage. The pilot's leg had suffered devastating injuries on impact, so it took some time to package and remove him. During the extrication process, I began to feel a burning sensation on my feet and lower legs and the stinging was getting worse by the minute. When the pilot had been removed, I began walking out of the marsh and onto firm land. I looked down to see my dress slacks were beginning to fall apart and my leather dress shoes were disintegrating. The aviation fuel was destroying my clothing and my feet felt as though they were on fire. I walked quickly to our engine, stripped down to my underwear and was decontaminated with water by a hand line from our engine. I stood there in my underwear in full view of motorists passing by on the highway. My lower legs and feet were cherry red from the aviation fuel that I had been trudging through. All those involved in the crash were hospitalized, but over time they would recover from their ordeal. I learned a valuable lesson that day. Never go anywhere without my bunker gear, which would have protected me from the aviation fuel.

Chapter 22

———— ❧ ————

THAT'S GOING TO
LEAVE A MARK

WHILE WORKING ON advancing my licensure level in EMS I had the opportunity to work rotations in the emergency room of a major trauma center. This is the last place on earth that most people would want to spend their time; however, for those of us who work in the field, the ER is an educationally enriched environment. There is so much to see and do while working alongside the doctors and nurses during some of the most chaotic and stressful times you can imagine.

It was a sunny fall Saturday afternoon and the ER was particularly quiet. I walked to the window overlooking the hospital complex and observed an ambulance making its way through the street with its emergency lights activated. I asked the charge nurse if we had received a patient radio report from an incoming unit. She said she had not been made aware of anything inbound. I told her that a rig (ambulance) was about to arrive at our door downstairs. She asked me to make a trauma room ready with IV lines and sterilized equipment while she summoned the attending physician. I readied the room to receive the patient as requested. Within minutes, the elevator doors opened and paramedics wheeled in their gurney. I directed them to the room I had set up. The charge nurse and attending physician came in right behind the gurney. The patient's entire head was wrapped in bandaging, with the exception of his nose. His appearance was like that of a mummy, except the wrapping around his head was saturated in blood.

I had already put on my gloves, when the doctor told me to stand by the patient's shoulder. We meticulously began to clip through the wrapped dressings around his face; one layer at a time. We would peel one back and then begin the next. When we had pulled back the last layer of bandaging and his face came into view, a nurse gasped at the sight of the man's disfigured face. He had been trimming a tree at his home and was attempting to remove a limb high above his head when the chainsaw he was holding suddenly kicked back, striking him directly in the face. The saw blade had struck him on the left side of the bridge of his nose at the edge of the eye socket. It continued in a downward path cutting through the maxilla (upper jaw), severing the mandible (lower jaw bone), and knocked out teeth on the upper and lower palates. The offset blades of the chainsaw had left a track about one quarter inch wide and it had gone nearly two inches deep before losing momentum.

The doctor asked me to get a step stool for his use. I rushed out of the room and returned with a step platform for him, setting it down on the floor near the patient's right shoulder. The doctor had a Polaroid camera and stepped onto the platform to snap a couple of pictures of the patient's face. I was asked to remove the patient's wallet from his denim slacks and withdraw the driver's license from his wallet. I realized that the doctor was obtaining a before and after likeness of the patient for the surgeons who would later be working on reconstructing his face. The young man had been administered several milligrams of morphine through an IV access, while being transported to help ease the pain. He was conscious but lethargic. His vital signs had remained stable throughout the transport.

The attending physician made a call for a surgical team to be assembled, and within a few minutes an RN and I rolled his bed to the surgical unit, where he was turned over to the surgical prep team. One week later, I returned to the ER for another rotation. The same charge nurse was on duty and I asked if she could provide me some follow-up on the chainsaw accident victim we had the previous week.

She asked, "Do you remember what time you took him upstairs?"

I said, "Yes, it was about 4:00 p.m." She told me that surgeons had worked in four-hour shifts throughout the night and into the next day to repair the damage. They reconstructed the lacrimal (tear) ducts, nerves to the mouth, the jaw bones, eye socket, as well as his nearly severed tongue. She said that the surgery went well, but he would require a lot of plastic surgery in order to reconstruct his face to look like he did before the accident.

Chapter 23

WOULD YOU MIND
GIVING ME A HAND?

A STATE POLICE fire investigator had just completed his training program and was assigned to our area of the state. My name had been provided to him by his predecessor as a possible resource to help him in his first few investigations until he was comfortable investigating on his own. I received a call from him one afternoon and he told me a structure fire had taken place the night before. He asked me if I would consider working with him on doing the investigation. I told him I would be happy to assist him.

He thanked me and said, "Why don't you meet me here in my office tomorrow morning at 9 o'clock and we'll have coffee and head out to the scene."

I told him that sounded fine. I arrived a little before nine the next morning and we sat down and got to know each other over coffee. As we chatted, his office phone rang. He answered and grabbed a note pad. He asked the caller where the fire had occurred and how much the insured value of the structure was. He hesitated and said, "Well, my partner and I were just about to head out to investigate an apartment fire. Hang on a second." He placed his hand over the phone and said, "A large fire took place early this morning. It was a manufacturing facility valued at well over a million dollars and it needs to be investigated. What do you think?"

I replied, "I'm in."

He got on the phone and said, "Alright, my partner and I will get on the road. Give me the address."

We loaded my equipment into the state-owned van and headed out. Our trip toward the west side of the state took nearly an hour and a half. We arrived to be greeted by another state fire investigator who would work with us. I knew him through my affiliation and attendance at annual fire investigation programs conducted around the state. We discussed how to go about the investigation, and they asked me if I would walk around obtaining statements from the owner, any witnesses that saw the fire and the local fire chief. I told them I was there to assist them in whatever capacity they deemed necessary. The two investigators put on coveralls, boots, and hard hats to begin the process of going through the rubble. Armed with note pad and pen, I began to interview people to glean information on how the fire might have started, where they first saw flames coming from the building, and other relevant information.

One citizen had videoed the fire from the roadway and I asked if I might see it. She was accommodating and showed me the video. It was very useful to the investigation because she had captured images of the fire when it first broke through the roofline. I obtained her name, phone number, and address, and explained that our team may wish to have a copy of her video. Many of those I spoke to had no pertinent information to the investigation. I found the local fire chief sitting on the tailboard of his fire engine, covered in soot, sweaty and exhausted. I introduced myself and told him I was assisting in the fire investigation. I asked him what time his department had received the 911 call, as well as their arrival time. He got on his radio and contacted his station for the time of call and arrival on scene. The information was relayed back to the chief.

I said, "This makes for a long day, Chief!"

He replied, "Yeah, but this wasn't the only call for service last night."

I said, "Really? What else did you have, Chief?"

He told me that just an hour or so before being dispatched to the industrial structure fire, they had gone to the local high school for activated smoke alarms. When they arrived, they found smoke in the computer lab. The wiring on the computers had melted and all the computers were damaged. I asked him if I could have his time out on that call as well. The owner of the building told me that he performed a walkthrough of his business after his employees had left and locked the building down. The doors were found locked after the fire.

I made my way back to the state investigators, who were standing outside taking a break. As I approached, one said, "Do you want to take a ride in the fire department's bucket truck? I would like to see the building from the air."

I said, "Sure."

We climbed into the bucket and the engineer slowly raised

us high above the ruins. I pointed to an area in the middle of the building's remains and told him, "I watched a video taken from a bystander just after fire broke through the roof and it was in this area."

He replied, "That makes perfect sense; that's the area which sustained the greatest damage."

We were lowered to the ground and I continued to gather information regarding witness statements, names, and phone numbers. About a half hour later, the state investigators called for me to join them in the middle of the building. I put on my boots and made my way to their location where they had been digging through the rubble. They had cleared an area of the concrete floor about twelve feet square. They showed me the building support beams had sustained deep burning all the way to the floor level. Low-level burning on a hard surface is a potential indicator of flammable liquids being present.

They returned to their investigation while I walked out to meet with the owner again. I asked him what type of process was used in the manufacturing. He explained that metal frames were constructed in the left third of the building; the frames were rolled into an area where liquid glue was applied when the roof section was assembled on the truck cap manufacturing process.

I thanked him and returned to the building. I went to an area not far from where the investigators had been digging. I found a large metal housing that had been crushed when the roof caved in. I found fire extinguishment nozzles and piping attached to the underside of the hood. I climbed over roof trusses to the back side of the shroud and found a fire extinguishment manifold system. A system such as this has a number of containers of firefighting agent stored under pressure.

When the temperature under the hood reaches a certain level, the system activates and floods the area with the extinguishing agent. I looked at the three cylinders and distribution system and found the containers full and pressurized. The fire had not caused the system to activate. The fire had been above the system and the roof collapsed resulting in the hood being crushed, but the system had not activated. I looked around the building and saw barrels lying on their sides with the lids off. On closer observation, I realized the drums had contained glue used in the laminating process of manufacturing.

I called out to the investigators and shared the information about the laminating process using hot glue under the fire extinguisher hood. I explained that the fire extinguishing system had not been activated. The extreme low-level burning along the floor was the result of overturned drums of glue burning. The drums of glue were knocked over and ignited from the burning roof falling from above.

One of the investigators remarked jokingly, "I wish you could have told us before we spent over an hour digging through the debris!"

I chuckled and said, "Guys, I'm sorry about that, but I just put this together. I do, however, have some interesting information to share with you. What would you think if I told you that a little over an hour before the fire department was called to this address, they were at the high school for a smoke investigation? The computer lab suffered significant damage to the computers and their cords were melted."

We looked at each other and the lead investigator remarked, "This sounds like it might be a power surge!"

We walked out of the building and found the electrical feed coming into the site. The conduit came up through the concrete floor in the northeast corner and ran the entire length of the building along the upper wall. We secured the assistance of a fireman, using a circular saw with a gasoline motor, called a K-12 in the fire service. He cut sections of the electrical conduit about five feet in length and let them fall to the floor. We pulled away each section and inspected the wiring inside. We found that the wiring inside the conduit had been heated to the point that the protective sheathing had melted, causing puddling inside the conduit. This was a very important finding, given the fact that this area of the building had not suffered flame damage which would have caused the wire coatings to melt.

As we continued to make our way across the wall, we saw an area of heavy wood charring that went from an electrical outlet near the floor and went all the way to the roof. The outlet was heavily burned, the wires bare of insulation We asked the owner what process took place at this point of production. He told us that wooden cross sections were cut using a table saw. Further investigation determined that a power surge had occurred, which resulted in igniting a pile of sawdust that had accumulated near the outlet. The flames traveled up the wall to the roofline and spread horizontally. This was the area identified in the video that showed the flames coming through the roof early in the fire. There is a saying in the fire service: "Fire burns up, buildings burn down." The fire was determined to be the result of a power surge to the building.

Chapter 24

No Way Out

THE FIRE DEPARTMENT was dispatched for a report of a deceased subject inside his home. A request went out for additional manpower to report to the station to assist. I was in my private vehicle and drove normal traffic to the scene. I called the station and requested my gear be loaded on a truck for me. As I arrived, I walked to the home and saw my chief appear from the back of the home. He motioned with his hand for me to join him. He and I walked back around the home and he said, "Well, take a look inside and tell me how you think we should handle it."

I stood on my toes so I could peer into the window. I was looking into a bedroom, the decedent was lying on his back in bed. The individual was a very rotund person in life. The summer heat and four to five days since his passing had resulted in the swelling of the body to enormous proportions. To further add to the situation, the owner had several large dogs that had been trapped inside the home with him. They had deposited their bodily excretions all throughout the home, making an unbearable stench.

I said, "Chief, we're going to need SCBA (self-contained breathing apparatus) before we do anything."

We walked back to the front of the home where I began to get a breathing apparatus off the fire engine. The dispatch center had been calling local funeral directors for advice on how we might handle the situation. As I was suiting up, a local funeral director I knew arrived and walked to the back of the home with my chief. Moments later, the two reappeared and walked out to the front yard.

The funeral director saw me, came over, and shook my hand. He said, "Curt, I've been in the funeral business for sixteen years and I've never seen anything like this."

I replied, "Well, I've been in the fire service for over twenty-two years, and I've never had to deal with a situation quite like this either."

After discussing the situation with our medical director and with input from a family member, we were able to put an action plan in place. I suggested to my chief that we use a chain saw to make vertical cuts on the back wall as wide as the bed, and one horizontal cut above the window, and drop that section of the wall outward onto the ground. We would then enter the bedroom, carefully wrap the deceased in vinyl tarps, and seal the tarps with duct tape. Once the body was wrapped and sealed, we would lower it to the floor and bring it out. There was only one problem with our plan. There was no funeral facility that would accept the body. After a period of time, we were informed that a crematorium would receive the remains. With the approval of the family member, our plan was put in motion. A team of firefighters, wearing full turnout gear with air packs, entered the room and carried out the process of packaging the decedent. Once that was accomplished, they brought the body out on the wall section and placed it in the back of a fire department pickup truck with a cap on it. The side windows were darkened so no one could see inside. The remains were taken to the crematorium about an hour away.

We used strict site control to prevent onlookers from seeing what was happening. We treat everyone with respect and decorum, regardless of the circumstances of their passing, because they are someone's family member.

Chapter 25

I Will See You When You Get Home

It was 3:45 p.m. on a Friday afternoon when a 911 call was placed by our dispatch center to a vehicle crash about two miles from our station. I climbed into the command seat of our rescue unit. A member of the department drove who had only been with the department a few months. We rolled out of the station as our engine crew was assembling. As we arrived at the scene, the first thing I saw was a school bus sitting on the side of the highway with the emergency flashers activated. My driver parked a distance from the bus as I directed. I climbed from my seat and walked toward the bus; I saw a semi-tractor ahead of the parked bus in the opposite lane. A small pickup truck had crossed the centerline and was struck broadside by the semi-truck. A victim was draped over the driver's door, hanging from his torso, face down.

I yelled at the driver of the school bus, "Get those kids out of here!" The bus was loaded with children on their way home. They were lined up, staring at the pickup truck through the bus windows. The driver put the bus in gear and pulled away quickly.

I approached the pickup and checked for signs of life on the man hanging from the driver's door. I looked inside and realized that a second occupant was lying beneath the first victim. I yelled to my driver to come and aid me in lifting the first victim so I could see if the second victim was alive. He was frozen in his tracks. He had never been on the scene of a serious accident, let alone one with someone killed.

I yelled again, "I need your help, you've got to give me a hand!" He reluctantly approached and helped me lift the victim so I could reach into the driver's compartment and check for signs of life on the second man. Unfortunately, he was gone also. The engine crew arrived on the scene and I instructed personnel to get a sheet and cover the driver's side of the vehicle so passing motorists were prevented from seeing the body. I told my personnel to begin directing traffic to flow, because both lanes were backing up with vehicles. I made a radio call and informed our dispatch center that we had a double fatality crash and requested the state police for investigation. State troopers arrived and began to take pictures of the crash scene, which included numerous photos of the pickup, semi, and skid marks made from the pickup leading to the point of impact. In the back of the pickup box there was a deformed metal lunch box that had been forcibly opened by the collision. Lying in the bottom of the lunch box was a note left by the wife of the driver, which read: "I'll see you when you get home, I love you!"

When the troopers had gathered everything they needed,

they authorized the removal of the victims. A wrecker was then put in place to take the truck to a secured location for further examination. The semi-tractor had sustained little damage and was still roadworthy. However, in light of the traumatic situation the driver had just gone through, the truck was parked farther down the road in a parking lot, and another driver was sent to make the remainder of the haul. Back at the station I spoke with my driver and asked him if he was alright. He told me that he had never experienced death and he was shocked by what he saw. I told him I felt bad about putting him in that situation but I had no alternative. I told him, "Unfortunately, in this line of work we're going to see these types of incidents. You never get used to it; let your training take over, do what you are trained to do and learn to control your emotions."

I told him if he ever wanted to talk to me about the incident or any other incident, I would always be there for him.

Chapter 26

I'm Glad You Don't Hold A Grudge!

IN THE LATE evening hours, the fire department received a call for a snowmobiler who had driven his machine into open water in the middle of an area lake. We responded to the lakeshore and tried to hear or visualize the downed snowmobiler. It was wintertime and very cold and windy. He was a long way from the shoreline. We commandeered a flat-bottom duck boat from a neighbor's yard. We tied lengths of rescue rope to the watercraft and two firefighters climbed in. Slowly they forced their way through the ice by breaking it up with a tool they had with them; soon they were out of sight. As the officer in charge, I had a knot in my stomach over my concern for the safety of my rescue team.

Our police chief stood by me and I shared my sense of

dread. I told him, "There's a better and safer way to make these types of water extractions without risking the lives of our firemen."

He replied, "How is that?"

I said, "A hovercraft."

"A what?" he exclaimed.

I said again, "A hovercraft. With all the lakes we have in the area, we should have a hovercraft for situations just like this."

Eventually, our rescue team would call back to the shore command to slowly retrieve them with the rope. I feared that at any moment the now overloaded watercraft could be overturned, throwing my men into the icy waters. My fears were proven unfounded moments later when the boat carrying the victim and our rescue team came into view. The snowmobiler would be taken ashore and treated for hypothermia. He came through the ordeal just fine. Our rescue team members, cold, wet and exhausted, returned home to get out of their wet clothes and get a hot shower. The mission was a success, and a life had been saved!

Over the course of the winter, I continued to dwell on that night and the concerns I had for the safety of our department members. I considered how we could fund the purchase of a hovercraft, which I felt in my heart was the right way to confront those types of rescues. I began to put together a plan to fund the purchase of the specialized equipment. I organized a demonstration of a hovercraft and invited members of our governing body to watch. The pilot showed the craft's ability to fly from land onto open water and back again. He answered several questions about the craft and it's capabilities from our board members and then asked them if they would like to go for a ride. Several members took him up on the offer and I

MEMOIRS OF MAYHEM

believe they recognized the lifesaving capability that the craft could provide. At a board meeting sometime later, we proposed the purchase of a hovercraft. However, it was met with a mixed response. The fire budget could not fund the purchase; however, with much discussion, the board would provide a portion toward the cost if we could somehow come up with the remaining money.

I began to reach out to property owners' associations from all across our community and asked to be placed on their annual meeting agenda. As I waited for these upcoming meetings, I put together a presentation which showcased hovercraft vehicles used in rescue work. My presentation highlighted the number of lakes in our jurisdiction and our rescue responsibilities. In the following months, I made my pitch to the property owners' groups and was even invited to make a presentation to several area private businesses. Much to our delight, checks began to arrive earmarked for the rescue craft from these organizations and businesses. As the funding for the craft continued to grow, I began to write the specifications and an equipment list for the craft. When the funding reached within five thousand dollars of the purchase, we approached our board to allow us to place the purchase order.

The board members were somewhat concerned since all the funds had not been raised, but they were also surprised that we had managed to raise so much money so quickly. The board voted to write the purchase order.

With a purchase order in place, the company owner began to install the V-6 power plant, controls, light bar, siren, and quartz halogen light bar for visibility for night operations. The hovercraft rescue vehicle was paid for and delivered in late August. The manufacturer spent a day with us on a lake getting us familiarized with the craft's operation. It's much different from operating any other vehicle. There was much training and practice needed to become proficient with the craft before winter came. Training with the hovercraft continued into the winter months so we were familiar with its operation on ice. By it's nature, the craft flies faster on a hard surface than on open water.

I was sitting in a board meeting one evening about the third week of March when a call came in for a subject through the ice on one of our lakes. I bolted from the meeting, got into my car, and headed toward the fire station. I got on my portable radio and told the station I would meet them at an intersection on the way to the scene. I parked my car and hopped aboard our brush truck, which served as the tow vehicle for the trailer on which the hovercraft was loaded.

I told my driver when we arrived, "Just park on the roadway, I will fly the craft off the trailer to the shoreline."

As we approached our launch site, one of our members radioed me; he was positioned on the opposite side of the lake from where we were and he could see an overturned watercraft. He said he would shine his flashlight and I needed to fly the craft toward his light to locate our victim. My assistant chief climbed aboard as I got the craft off the trailer and onto the snow-covered ground. I twisted the throttle, the craft lifted itself up, and we took off toward our firefighter's light beam. The high-intensity flying lamps lit the way to the middle of the lake. There had been several attempts to throw rescue objects to the subject, but he was too far out to reach with ropes, throwing rings, and tree branches. By the time we reached the individual, he had been in the water over fifteen minutes and I knew he was going to be very hypothermic in the icy waters. I brought the craft carefully to the side of the overturned canoe and all I saw was a face above the water level. Fortunately, the man realized that he would succumb to hypothermia and lose consciousness. He had placed his arm under and around a seat support and locked his wrist on the outer edge of the hull of the canoe, which held him afloat.

My assistant chief removed his arm from its locked position as I reached over the side of the craft and grabbed him by the collar of his water-laden coat and snatched him out of water. With my partner's aid, we lowered him onto the hovercraft. Only then did I recognize this man as my former high school teacher. We bundled him up with a blanket for transport to shore.

Our 911 center called my assistant chief on the radio and asked if he would like to scramble the county dive team. He replied, "Negative, we have a live rescue."

I jumped back on the seat and navigated the craft to shore where an ambulance team stood by ready to care for him. I lifted him and handed him to the paramedics, when a neighbor said, "What about the dog?"

I said, "What dog?"

The neighbor said she had called the owner and told him the dog was barking from the middle of the lake. The owner grabbed his canoe from the storage shed and began forging his way across the broken ice floes toward his dog when his canoe flipped over tossing him into the icy water as well. I turned the craft toward the middle of the lake and accelerated back to the overturned canoe. I set the craft alongside it and tilted the canoe halfway upright. There in the nose of the canoe was the Dalmatian, hanging on for dear life to a brace in the bow. I pulled the canoe alongside the hovercraft until the dog was within reach and pulled him to the safety of the rescue craft. We wrapped him up, flew back to shore where a local veterinarian stood by to take him to his clinic for observation and treatment. The hovercraft, which had only been a thought a year before, had saved the life of a man in our community, who was respected and loved by all, along with his Dalmatian sidekick.

The following morning, I was awakened by the sound of my phone ringing. I rolled over and grabbed the phone and answered. The caller identified himself and said, "We are live on the radio." He said he would like to ask me about our lifesaving rescue from the previous night. While still trying to get myself fully awake, the reporter interviewed me as I lay in my bed.

In the weeks that followed, the life saving rescue received much publicity. Later on, I was contacted by a producer from the Discovery Channel. He expressed an interest in coming to the United States from the UK to film an episode for their TV series titled "Extreme Machines." They wanted to highlight the rescue mission. They brought a film crew over to recreate that eventful evening. The episode was aired many times. The rescue of my former teacher was one of many lifesaving missions we performed with the craft. Quite some time had passed when I happened to cross paths with him again. We chatted and laughed together.

I asked him, "Do you remember the day you put me in a storage closet in the front of the classroom for talking in class?" Of course, I was guilty as charged!

He smiled and said, "Yes I do Curt, and I'm really glad you didn't hold a grudge!"

Chapter 27

—◆◆◆—

I'LL CALL YOU IF I NEED YOU!

I WAS BREAKING in a new partner with the EMS agency. I drove him around our response area so he could become acclimated to our response area. I took him around to a few of our lake communities, which could be confusing. It was an extremely hot and humid August day. The lakes were covered with boaters, jet skis, and swimmers. I had taken him around two lakes and was showing him a densely populated area of summer cottages when we rolled up on a man who was trimming his hedges in front of his neatly kept cottage. He was a very rotund gentleman, probably in his seventies, chewing on a cigar. He was sunburned and sweating profusely from his activities. I stopped the rig, rolled down my window and struck up a conversation. I told him it was far too hot for him to be working in the mid-day heat. I informed him it would be better if he got in the shade and took it easy until the temperature cooled off before finishing his task. He said he was just about done and didn't want to put if off.

I said, "Be careful."

He jokingly replied, "Don't worry! I'll call you if I need you!" I waved, rolled up my window, and continued on.

We completed the tour of the lake community and began making our way out onto the main highway. The local fire department was dispatched for a possible cardiac arrest. The 911 center gave the fire department the street name and address. I stopped the rig and began turning around.

My new partner asked, "Where are we're going?"

I replied, "You know the guy trimming his hedges?"

"Oh no!" he said.

Our dispatcher gave us the call; however, I was already headed in that direction. Now, with lights and siren activated, we hastened to the address. When we arrived in front of the home, fire-rescue was performing CPR on the man in the yard; his hedge trimmers lay by his side. It had not been more than fifteen minutes prior that he and I had been visiting. The fire department assisted in getting him on a long back board and on to the ambulance gurney. A good friend of mine from the department climbed into the back of the rig and assisted me as we continued to work on our patient as we made our way to the hospital. Unfortunately, the patient did not survive the cardiac emergency.

Chapter 28

TRAGEDY AT THE TRACK

PROVIDING RESCUE AND fire protection at Michigan International Speedway during race events were always busy times for those of us working in emergency services. With well over one hundred thousand fans in attendance during NASCAR's heyday, we would respond to chest pains, heat exhaustion, cardiac arrests, falls, heat stroke, severe intoxication, diabetic emergencies, and many various types of calls for service. At one time, those attending race events at MIS would make the gathering the fifth-largest population in the state. Being a part of emergency services at the track for nearly twenty years our members had seen a lot, however, what we were about to experience on this day was nothing like we had ever seen before.

The race was the US 500, open wheel, Indy cars racing under the Championship Auto Racing Teams or (CART) sanctioning body. The Indy cars provided some of the most exciting racing anywhere, with speeds reaching in excess of two hundred miles per hour. The race had gone 175 laps of the 250 scheduled laps around the two-mile oval when disaster struck. One of the cars came out of turn four, lost control, and slammed into the barrier in front of the grandstands. The impact caused the right front tire assembly to be severed from the car. It flew over a retaining fence and into the grandstands.

I was functioning as the operations chief. My radio came to life and the control tower called, gave us a grandstand section number, and exclaimed, "Roll! Roll! Debris in the grandstands!"

We began making our way across the back of the stands with sirens and air horns blaring to clear pedestrians from our path. As we arrived at the area, I made my way into the stands against a surge of hysterical race fans who were pushing each other to get out. Our crew members followed my lead into the stands. I pointed and indicated where the injured were located. Our members began fanning out to assess and treat those who had been injured. As I made my way up, I saw two spectators who were deceased. Our agency was assisted by paramedical ambulance staff and several members of the track staff. The injured were quickly treated and transported for further care at the infield care center and an area hospital. Everyone who took part worked as a team to rapidly triage, treat, and transport those injured. We provided assistance by holding up sheets around the site while the investigation took place to prevent the news media from capturing images. I asked a MIS staff member to acquire several bottles of bleach and a couple long-handled scrub brushes to use for the cleaning and disinfecting the grandstands. I sent a message to our station to bring a supply of disposable one piece protective suits, gloves, and face shields for personnel that would assist in the cleanup efforts.

During the disinfecting process, a track representative called to me from the bottom of the grandstand and asked me to come down. I said, "Alright, but I need to go through decontamination before I can speak to anyone."

I climbed down the stairway, went through the decontamination line, removed my soiled garments, and applied sanitizer to my hands. I hastily put on my uniform shirt and walked toward the back of the grandstands. A man was standing beside a sedan and as I got closer, I recognized an executive member of the track. He shook my hand and said, "Curtis, I want you to express my sincere thanks to all of your personnel for doing what you're doing." He spoke softly and his voice cracked with emotion. "I could have never dreamed that something like this would ever happen."

He shook my hand, thanked me again, and slowly walked away. I could sense the pain and anguish he was feeling in the aftermath of the darkest day in the history of the track. Late that evening, everyone who had taken part during the emergency—firefighters, ambulance staff, grandstand ushers, infield hospital staff, and maintenance staff—all took part in a Critical Incident Stress Debriefing in one of the buildings on site. CISD is a crisis intervention method that addresses overwhelming effects which first responders sometimes feel. Many of those involved were trying to cope with the aftermath of this very tragic event.

Chapter 29

UNWRITTEN RULES OF EMS

THERE IS AN unwritten list of do's and don'ts when working EMS units. The first on the list of don'ts is: Don't pass up the opportunity to go to the bathroom. Even if you haven't got the slightest feeling of needing to go, if the opportunity presents itself, GO! The next time you have an opportunity may be hours away. Do grab a bite to eat whenever you have the chance, even if not officially time to eat. I recall one evening working a unit when we completed a run and swung by a local restaurant to have a bite around 6:00 p.m. Just as we pulled into the parking lot, we got our next call. Our next attempt would be approximately 8:00 p.m. We pulled into the parking lot and walked to the door only to get hit again. After that call was completed, we drove to the restaurant and parked the bus, walked inside, had a seat, and placed our order. As we waited, we received another call. We told the waitress to stop our order as we headed to the door. Hungry and exhausted after the call, we drove back one more time in an attempt to get something to eat. We walked to the door, found it to be locked with a closed sign hanging in the window. It was now 10:10 p.m.

Dejected, we began walking back to our rig when someone yelled out: "Hey, come back here. We'll get you guys something to eat!" Bless the owner for his willingness to feed us despite the fact they had already closed for the evening. I will always remember his act of kindness.

On another night we drove through a fast-food chicken restaurant and placed an order for two chicken dinners with mashed potatoes, gravy, cole slaw and a biscuit. No sooner had they placed the boxed dinners in my partner's hand than we were dispatched to an emergency call. The location of an automobile crash was about six miles away. My partner was at the wheel; I activated the emergency lights and siren. When we arrived on scene, I was wiping my hands with a pre-moistened hand wipe and the box was empty except a few chicken bones. Mission accomplished!

I believe that working EMS is why I tend to eat so fast, much to my wife's displeasure.

Don't ever utter the words, "It sure is quiet." You can think it, but for heaven's sake, don't say it! If you do, you can probably forget about getting any sleep during the shift. Do not volunteer to take a shift swap for a crew member when the shift falls on a full moon. If you do have to work it, get lots of rest the night before. If a full moon should happen to fall on a Friday the 13th, well, good luck with that! Lastly, do not get on the wrong side of your dispatcher! If you do, when they have an opportunity, they can and will get even!

Chapter 30

A Gut Feeling

EARLY IN MY EMS career I was working a Basic Life Support (BLS) unit with a female partner. We had just completed the transfer of a patient to an area hospital. We disinfected our cot, changed the linen, and completed our paperwork. I climbed into the driver's seat, started the engine, dropped it in gear, and gunned it out of the parking lot.

My partner said, "What's the hurry?"

I said, "Something just happened!"

"What just happened?" she said.

"I don't know, but we need to get back to our district." She looked at me as if I were crazy; however, less than a half mile from the hospital our radio came to life. Our dispatcher advised us of a serious injury accident on the state highway. I engaged our emergency warning systems and put the accelerator to the floor.

My partner said, "Alright, this is scary." The conversation stopped at that point as I was completely focused on driving. The road conditions were clear and dry, which aided us in our response time to the scene. We arrived just behind the local fire department and parked. Suddenly my driver's door was pulled open and a wide-eyed firefighter grabbed me by my duty jacket and began pulling me out of my seat with my seatbelt still in place.

He was nearly hysterical as he yelled, "Hurry, you've got to help him."

I jumped from the unit and was pulled to a drainage ditch alongside of the roadway. Lying in the ditch, with lower extremities in water and icy slush, was a young man who was unconscious and had suffered a mid-thigh amputation of his leg. I grabbed a tourniquet from my pocket and applied it above the amputation site. I told firemen to assist my partner in getting the cot out. We placed the man on the cot and loaded him in the back. We placed him on 100% oxygen with a nonrebreather mask, applied MAST (Military Anti-Shock Trousers) pants, and inflated the unaffected leg and abdominal sections of the device. I instructed my partner to get me to the hospital ASAP. Once we were underway, I got on the radio and provided the nature of the injury, what we had done, and reported a blood pressure of 60 with shock pants inflated. I asked that a helicopter be dispatched to meet us at the hospital.

The ER doctor responded rather sarcastically, "Well, thank you very much but I'll make that decision after I've seen the patient."

I jerked my headset off and threw it against the wall in frustration. We arrived at the hospital, unloaded the patient, and rushed through the door of the emergency room. The nurses were ready and began starting two IV lines and retaking vitals. There had been no change in his condition since we applied the MAST trousers.

The attending physician strolled into the exam room and stopped just inside the doorway. He looked at the young man lying on the gurney, spun around, and rushed out. I stepped away and followed the doctor into the nurse's station where he was on the phone. I heard him say, "We have a serious trauma patient who's suffered a mid-thigh amputation of his leg. How fast can your helicopter get here?"

My blood was near boiling point when he hung up the telephone. The doctor turned to find me standing in front of him. I stuck my finger toward his face and said, "That helicopter could be here right now if you had not been so high and mighty." He put his hands up in an attempt to stop me. I continued, "Have I ever lied to you about a patient? Have I ever given you a bad patient assessment?" He said I hadn't. "Then why didn't you order the chopper when I requested it? Is it that you wanted to let everyone know that you're large and in charge?"

He waved his hands in my face and walked away, saying, "This is not the time."

I stopped and realized that I had been yelling; no one was moving or saying a word. When I walked out my partner was standing in the hallway, her eyes wide in disbelief.

We collected our equipment and began the process of cleaning our unit and getting it resupplied for the next run. My partner said, "I just want you to know that I agree with you all the way, but I've never seen a doctor get verbally dressed down like that before."

We went back to our crew quarters and prepared to get

some sleep. My mind was racing. I was trying to calm myself down when out of the darkness I heard my partner say, "So how often do you get one of those feelings?"

I said, "It's only happened a few times."

She replied, "Well, that's good."

I said, "But you know what? When I get one, it's never wrong!"

I fully expected to be terminated by my employer for my actions that night. However, the doctor never filed a complaint against me. Perhaps, after thinking it over, he felt he deserved it.

A few weeks later my partner and I were presented a letter from the ambulance service owner that he received from the trauma surgeon who worked on the young man. He credited us for saving the young man's life by our rapid intervention. While I regret blowing up that night, I do not tolerate arrogance that could affect a patient's life.

In emergency medicine, we have to be team players. Team members must trust each other's judgment, for the good of our patients. My outburst in the emergency room was never brought up in future conversations between the physician and myself.

Chapter 31

WHERE THERE IS SMOKE, YOU'LL FIND FIRE

I WAS WORKING an ALS unit in the city and my partner and I were rolling along a street where a large metal salvage yard is located. We were idly chatting. As we passed I noticed light smoke drifting up from behind the facility maintenance shop. I turned, looked over my shoulder, glanced back, and called to my partner to stop and turn around. I told him, "There's smoke showing from the salvage yard."

He replied, "We're not in the firefighting business." and continued to drive. I yelled and told him to turn the rig around. We needed to investigate where the smoke was coming from, because the business was closed at the time. Reluctantly, he made a U-turn at the next intersection and drove down the service drive. The plume of smoke had grown larger by the time we turned the corner of the building. What we saw burning were metal contents in an open-top semi-trailer. The metal was mounded above the side rails of the semi trailer and heavy smoke was being generated from within. I knew from my firefighting background that ordinary metals do not burn. However, there are a few that will, including magnesium and the trailer was full of it. I exited the rig to get a closer look and saw that the aluminum underbelly of the trailer was getting hot. I ran back to the ambulance and told my partner to call dispatch and have them request the fire department for a metal fire at the salvage yard. He grabbed the radio and relayed the information. As I watched, the fire and smoke continued to intensify. The underbelly of the tanker began to turn red from the heat being generated.

My partner, who wanted nothing to do with investigating the source of the smoke, was now out of our rig with his 35-millimeter camera in hand, taking photographs of this trailer from every angle. I noticed that the semi-trailer was resting directly over a large water puddle and yelled at my partner to withdraw. I told him that when the fire melted through the bottom of the trailer and the hot metal came in contact with the water, it would spew hot burning material in all directions. He backed away and we watched as the belly and side of the trailer got so hot that it became translucent; we could actually see through it.

I heard the siren of the fire engine getting closer as we continued to watch. The fire engine rolled in and took a position well behind the burning trailer. The officer in charge was a captain with the department. As he approached us, I said, "Captain, you've got your work cut out for you! You've got a whole trailer load of magnesium burning!"

He replied, "Oh shit!" He grabbed his portable radio and requested a second engine company dispatched to our location. No sooner had he completed his radio transmission than the molten metal made it's way through the bottom of the trailer. As the metal began to fall into the water, it sprayed out in all directions like lava spewing from a volcano. My partner was completely engrossed in what was taking place and continued to capture images of the fiery metal being blown into the air. The fire department was quickly getting their foam equipment ready to spray on the trailer when the tires on the trailer began to explode from the intense heat. The second engine arrived on the scene and provided additional containers of foam to be applied to the trailer. We got back in the ambulance and continued to watch their suppression efforts for a few moments before pulling away and heading to our crew quarters.

My partner talked about the fire off and on throughout the day. He couldn't wait to get this camera film developed. I had seen small amounts of magnesium burn before, but nothing of that magnitude. It was like watching fireworks on the Fourth of July!

Chapter 32

A REVERSAL IN ROLES

IT WAS A beautiful summer morning, my partner and I had completed the equipment inventory and made sure all critical equipment performed as needed. We gave our rig a bath and had breakfast when the phone rang in our modest crew quarters. Our dispatcher provided an address to one of the many lakes in our area. She told us there had been a boating accident with one injury. When we arrived, we were directed to our patient by bystanders along the way. We made our way down a hill behind a cottage to the boat dock, where our patient was lying on his back, with several people gathered around. As we stepped onto the dock, people began to spread to the sides making way for my partner and me.

I knelt down next to the man, introduced myself, and told him we were there to treat him. His right leg had been wrapped in beach towels and ice from the mid-calf level down to his toes. The towels were saturated in blood. I asked what had happened and he told me he had been swimming along the shoreline when he heard a speed boat approaching from behind. He said he rolled toward his side to look back and saw the bottom of a boat rapidly heading directly toward him. He dove head first into the lake to prevent being struck by the boat's propeller; however, he didn't completely get out of the way, resulting in his lower leg being struck.

As he was providing me the details of the incident, I had been getting my protective gloves on, and my partner was connecting and flushing two IV lines. The gentleman said, "There is something you need to know about me before you do anything."

I said, "Yes sir, what is that?"

He informed me that he was a trauma surgeon from a very prestigious and nationally recognized medical center. I stared at the man lying in front of me and I glanced over to his wife who was standing in the water with her arms folded neatly on the deck alongside her husband and I said, "So, Doctor, what you're really saying is, today is not the day to screw up!"

He sternly replied, "You've got that right, Mister!"

I said, "All right, sir, I'll keep that in mind."

I told him I was going to examine his right leg and foot as I began carefully pulling back the beach towels which had been placed around his leg. When I removed the towels, which had been packed in ice, I saw that his right foot was nearly severed from the leg about four inches above the ankle. In fact, the only thing holding the foot to his leg was a portion of skin tissue. The boat propeller had sliced through muscle, blood vessels, tendons, and bone.

I placed the towel back in place and he asked me, "Well, what do you think?"

I turned and said, "Well, Doc, I think you're going to have to get some stitches,"

His wife giggled nervously, but the doctor found no humor and said, "Oh, great! I've got a comedian working on me." Levity is sometimes used in some situations like this, but it wasn't working here! I told him that we were going to start bilateral IV lines and he said, "Why? I don't need an IV." I asked him to hold his hands in front of his face and tell me what color they were. He did so and he said, "Well, they're kind of white."

I replied, "Yes they are, the same color as your face and the rest of your body. Doctor, I understand that you have a vast amount of training and experience, but today you're the patient, and I'm in charge."

"Fine!" he retorted. I placed a tourniquet above his left elbow, sanitized the joint in preparation for the IV needle insertion, removed a fourteen-gauge IV needle from its package, and turned to him and said, "You know, Doc, since we are being completely candid with each other, there is something you should know about me."

He said, "What's that?"

I said, "I have never done this before."

He said, "Good Lord man! you've never started an IV?"

I said, "Oh sure, I've started hundreds of them but this is the first time I've ever stuck one in a doctor."

I inserted the needle in one swift motion, then connected the IV tubing and secured it in place. My partner started a second IV in his other arm. He was placed on oxygen and administered medication for pain management. We then focused on immobilizing the foot for transport. The method of choice was a ladder splint we carried on our rig. Once we had everything in order, we carried him on our stretcher to our ambulance. I contacted our medical control to provide a patient update which included prior care, vitals, and information about the near amputation of the right foot. I suggested to the ER physician that a surgical reattachment team would be needed or the patient might possibly need to be air lifted to a trauma center.

She thanked me and said she would be expecting us in approximately fifteen minutes. We arrived at the hospital and took the good doctor into the ER where we were directed to the trauma room. ER staff assisted us in transferring him from our gurney onto the hospital bed. The attending physician came in; she introduced herself, and I introduced our doctor patient to her. Our patient told the attending physician that he thought I had overstepped my boundaries by dictating instructions to her.

As a testament to the kind of physician she was, she told the patient, "Curtis provided clear, concise details regarding your condition and provided options in a timely manner." She went on to say that since I was quick to get on the radio and give her the details, she had scrambled a surgical reattachment team and they were in the process of scrubbing up and getting ready for him in a surgical suite.

Our patient said, "Well, I can't say a lot about his bedside manner, but he did do a heck of a job out there."

Our attending physician said, "I would expect nothing less." giving me a wink!

Our patient shook our hands and thanked us for our care.

We departed the room to begin the process of cleaning the rig and writing reports. Upon follow-up with regard to our patient's condition, we learned that the reattachment surgery was successful.

Chapter 33

PATIENT AND
CAREGIVER REUNION

LATE ONE EVENING while working on an advanced life support (ALS) unit we were dispatched to a report of a vehicle crash outside the city on a stretch of county road. As we made our way to the scene, we were given additional information that the crash was a head-on impact. When you respond to a crash of this nature, you never know what kinds of injuries you might be faced with. I've seen people walking around the crash site who had climbed out of their car with only scrapes and bruises. I've also seen deceased in the car or victims suffering from major traumatic injuries. It's something I could never understand or make sense of; how some die while others walk away unscathed.

As we rolled onto the crash site, what I saw was beyond

belief. In the roadway sat the frame and drive train of a car. The entire chassis of the vehicle had been sheared completely off and was lying on the opposite side of the road. I had never seen this before in all my years of working in emergency services. The second vehicle was crushed beyond recognition and had been kicked backward from the point of impact. Bystanders told us there were two victims and pointed in their direction. My partner and I separated to locate and begin treatment on the victims. One male was thrown from the impact into a corn field to the left side of the road. I grabbed a trauma bag from the unit and headed into the corn field with my mini mag flashlight to provide light. I found a young man lying on his back with serious facial lacerations, his face nearly unrecognizable.

Head and facial injuries bleed profusely due to the concentration of many small blood vessels, and while grotesque in nature, they are not necessarily life-threatening, unless the bleeding compromises the airway. The patient size-up begins with the fundamentals of care, the ABC's: airway, breathing, and circulation. When I had completed that, I began to look for potential life-threatening injuries such as bleeding into the abdomen or pelvic region, broken ribs and/or, closed or open chest wounds which could collapse the lungs, impairing the victim's ability to breathe. I also checked for broken bones of the extremities, and so on.

During my patient assessment, the young man began to regain consciousness and tried to speak. I identified myself and told him to take it easy and that I would take good care of him. I enlisted the aid of a bystander, who had just arrived, to retrieve an oxygen tank from our unit and bring it to me. I connected the tubing and mask to the tank, opened the valve to allow oxygen to flow into the mask, and placed it over his face. I grabbed a bag of IV solution, ripped it from its container, and plugged the IV delivery line into the bag. I handed the solution to a bystander while I flushed the air from the IV tubing. I quickly cleaned the fold of his elbow for the insertion of the IV needle. In the darkness of the corn field, with only a flashlight I held in my teeth for light, I guided the IV needle into his vein to allow the solution to make its way into his circulatory system.

The local fire department had arrived and came to aid me in caring for and preparing the patient for loading into the rig. My partner had previously called dispatch for a second unit to the scene. With two units now on site, we loaded both men for transport. I called the hospital and provided the charge nurse an assessment of my findings, a current set of vital signs, and our estimated time of arrival. We had hospital staff help us unload the patients. I told them that I needed to keep my hands on the patient's face.

We made our way into the ER and my patient was transferred to a hospital bed. Shortly, the attending physician came in to further assess the young man. I was standing at the head of the hospital bed with my hands holding a sterile dressing on the young man's face. The attending physician said, "Alright Curtis! You can let go now."

I shook my head, indicating no. He started to say it again, but I motioned with my head for him to come closer. The doctor leaned over in my direction, I leaned forward and whispered in his ear, "Doc, If I let go with my hand, the side of his face will fall off." I slowly released pressure of the side of his face and the doctor saw the entire side of the man's face begin to slide away.

The doctor said, "OK, why don't you just stay where you're at for the time being."

The following summer, I pulled into a gas station to fill our diesel tank. As I climbed out of the rig, a young man stepped out from the gas station and walked toward me. He smiled and said, "Hi, do you remember me?"

I stared at him for a moment and I saw multiple scars on the side of his face. I replied, "You know what? I think I do remember you."

He smiled and said, "I remember looking up at you in the back of the ambulance on the way to the hospital that night and recognized you when you pulled in."

I told him that he looked much better than the last time I had seen him. He laughed and said, "Yeah, I guess I do." He shook my hand and told me how much he appreciated my help and the words of comfort and encouragement I gave him that night on the way to the hospital. Rare moments such as those were the rewards of my job.

Chapter 34

FIREFIGHTER DOWN

My partner and I had made transport to a large hospital complex about forty miles away. As we were driving back, I saw a large black plume of smoke rising up in the distance. I pointed and said, "It looks like the whole city is on fire!" We had a radio which could receive fire department frequencies, so we quickly turned on their channel to listen in on the traffic. As we listened, we heard activation tones of multiple agencies being requested for mutual aid to the city department. "This is a big one!" I said. My partner pressed a little harder on the accelerator as we continued on our way. As we got closer, we could see thick black smoke rising hundreds of feet in the air. We made our way downtown to our crew quarters, which also contained our dispatch center. We parked the rig, stood outside, watched the smoke, and listened to the sounds of sirens and air horns that filled the evening air. The fire was only about ten blocks from our quarters. We walked inside and spoke to our dispatcher about the nature of the fire. She informed us which building was on fire. It was a large multiple-story structure located near the heart of the city. We stood there in silence listening to the radio traffic from the fire commander giving instructions to incoming apparatus on where to position themselves. The city aerial truck was in service, applying water to the burning building, and two more aerial trucks had been requested from other agencies.

The dispatch phone rang; she answered it and hung up the phone. The fire department dispatch called us to report to the scene for standby. We climbed into our unit and made our way to the area. We had to stop and remove barricades from our path that had been put in place to stop civilian traffic. We took up a position alongside a row of storefronts across the street from the fire. It was raging despite the efforts of several fire departments. Water was being put on the fire from aerial trucks as well as hand lines on the ground. As we watched, we heard the sound of a deep rumble inside the building. Seconds later, the sound of an air horn pierced the air, blasting a long solid tone. That was an alarm to all personnel to evacuate.

Firefighters began to move away from the building, when suddenly the outside wall came crashing down. There had been a firefighter sitting in front of the building with a coiled fire hose beneath him, spraying water on the fire. Upon hearing the evacuation alarm the firefighter stood up, turned and began to walk away from the building. As he did, the entire outer wall caved outward. The brick and concrete from the multiple story building created a giant wave and rolled across the open area. As the dust and smoke cleared from the collapsed building, the firefighter had disappeared. He had been buried beneath the rubble. A fire engine behind where he had been standing was thrown backward nearly twelve feet by the force of the wave of collapsing concrete and brick. Firefighters, police officers, my partner and I ran to where the firefighter had been; we all began pulling bricks and digging our way through the debris, trying locate the buried firefighter.

When he was found, we quickly placed him on a back board and resuscitative efforts were begun. He was carried from the debris and loaded into our unit. My partner, along with a firefighter, jumped into the back, and I climbed behind the wheel and we made our way to the hospital. He was rushed into the emergency room where efforts continued to revive him. I walked outside to the rig, overcome with emotion by what I had just witnessed. A sedan came flying into the hospital parking lot and came to a screeching halt.

A man jumped out, saw me, and ran in my direction. He exclaimed, "Is our firefighter alive?"

I hesitated and said, "Sir, you need to talk to the ER staff." He clutched my uniform shirt in his hands, pinned me to the side of the ambulance and yelled, "Is our firefighter alive or not?"

I grabbed his hands and replied, "Sir, it doesn't look good."

He turned and slowly walked into the hospital emergency entrance. I was later told that he was perhaps a member of the city government. The firefighter succumbed to his injuries.

Chapter 35

---⚬⚬⚬---

THE STORK NEEDS
ASSISTANCE!

ONE MORNING AFTER making shift change and readying our unit for service, my partner and I headed out for breakfast. As we sat eating, we received a call to an apartment for a woman in labor. As we got up to leave, a lady sitting near us over hearing our radio call said, "It sounds like the stork needs help." The apartment was not far from where we were and we were on the scene in two to three minutes. I grabbed a house kit and headed for the apartment stairs when I heard screams coming from above. I was climbing the stairs two at a time and turned into the open apartment door. A lady was sitting on the floor with her elbows resting on the edge of a sofa and the baby's head was already visible.I yelled, "Don't push, don't push!"

I dropped down beside her, taking a position to her left

side, grabbed a pair of gloves, put them on and slid a sterile sheet into position against her buttocks and said, "Alright, push!"

I put slight resistance on the baby's head (as we are trained to do) and with one push the baby cleared the birth canal and was lying on the sheet. My partner was entering the apartment and handed me the obstetric kit. I tore open the plastic bag, recovering the bulb syringe used to suction mucus from the baby's mouth and nose. The baby and the mother were both crying. A crying newborn is what first responders want to hear! I removed the umbilical clamps from the kit and locked them onto the umbilical cord. We're trained to hold the umbilical cord until it stops pulsating before the cord is cut separating the baby from the mother. I cut the cord and applied antibacterial ointment. The baby was placed in a thermal blanket to maintain it's body temperature then placed on the mothers chest for mom to hold. We covered the baby and mother with a blanket for transport to the hospital.

I contacted the hospital and notified them that we were in route with a mother and newborn and provided vitals to the attending physician. He instructed us to go directly to the labor and delivery floor, bypassing the emergency room. We took the elevator to the labor and delivery suite and were met by members of the staff. The newborn and mother were taken back to a room. My partner and I sat down to write up our report which documented everything we did on the scene, including vital signs for mother and baby girl.

A few moments later a nurse came out and said, "The mother wants a picture taken with you."

I walked into the room where mom was holding the baby in her arms and she was glowing with happiness. I sat beside the bed and the nurse took a picture of the three of us. She thanked me and I said, "You are very welcome. I'm glad we were able to assist."

As I stepped out of the room, I was met by an obstetrics doctor who was standing near the nurse's station. He said, "Can I speak to you alone for a moment?"

My mind was racing. I thought to myself, *It was a textbook delivery with no complications; what could he want to talk to me about?* I said, "Certainly, doctor."

When we cleared the area where people could hear us, he put his hand on my shoulder and said, "Listen! my colleagues and I make a lot of money delivering babies and if the word ever gets out how easy it is, I'm afraid we're out of business." He broke into a smile and said, "Congratulations, nice job out there."

The truth is, a normal delivery is not that difficult. However, when things go wrong, it will make the most seasoned EMS crew member's pulse and blood pressure skyrocket. A skilled OB doctor is invaluable in those cases.

On another occasion, we were called to a home for a report of a female in active labor. We rushed to the scene unassisted by fire/rescue. We ran upstairs to the bedroom with our equipment and found a lady pushing to deliver. My partner gloved up and got out the emergency obstetrics kit. He pulled back the covers and we saw a tiny leg protruding from the birth canal. This was one of those "holy crap" moments. A breech delivery is a true life-threatening event for the unborn baby. I ran down the stairs and pulled the stretcher back up. My partner had placed the mother on oxygen so the baby would not be deprived. We gently lifted the mother onto the gurney, strapped her in, carried her down the stairs and loaded her for transport.

My partner grabbed me by my shirt collar, pulled me close and said, "You get me to the hospital ASAP!" I jumped into the driver's seat and told my partner that I would contact the ER to provide them our status so he could give full attention to our patient. I notified the attending physician that we were inbound with a breech delivery with an ETA of fifteen minutes. I'm sure, for my partner in the back of the rig, those minutes seemed like an eternity.

I backed the rig up to the ER where hospital staff members were lined up to assist us in unloading our patient. She was wheeled into a treatment room and an emergency C-section was performed; within three minutes we heard the sounds of a newborn crying. Shortly, we heard the sounds of a helicopter outside on the landing zone. The flight team burst through the ER doors with an incubator unit for the baby for the flight to the children's hospital. In a matter of fifteen minutes, the baby had been delivered by caesarian section and rushed to a helicopter for transport to a definitive care facility. We would learn later that mother and baby were fine. Good communication, teamwork, and rapid intervention made the difference.

Chapter 36

CIRCLING THE DRAIN

WE HAD COMPLETED our first medical call of the day, when we received a call from our dispatcher for report of an unconscious subject. We were provided the address, which was less than a mile from our location. We engaged our emergency lights and siren and responded to the incident address. Upon our arrival, we observed a group of three men standing over a young man lying on the ground. We immediately began to obtain his vital signs. His respiratory and pulse rates were extremely slow. As we continued with our assessment, I asked who was in charge of the site.

I quickly glanced around and asked again, "Gentlemen, who is in charge here?"

One of the three said, "I am."

I asked, "What was this young man doing just prior to losing consciousness?"

The man said, "He was cleaning the inside of the tank." Pointing to a large above ground stainless storage tank a few feet away. "We found him like this and pulled him out of the tank through the open side hatch."

I asked, "What was in the tank?"

"It's empty."

I said, "What were the contents of the tank prior to being emptied?"

I was told that the tank had been previously used to store acetone. Acetone is a clear, highly flammable and volatile liquid. It is widely used as a paint and varnish remover. It is also used to make other chemicals, plastics, and consumer products. Exposure to concentrated vapors can cause dizziness, unconsciousness, and even death. As the conversation took place, the young man was intubated and I was administering 100% oxygen directly into his lungs. My partner had established an IV line and placed him on a cardiac monitor. The patient was in serious trouble from the high concentrations of vapor inside the tank he was cleaning. His respiratory and cardiac rate were greatly depressed. A situation refered to as circling the drain, or in other words, at death's door.

As my partner began to administer drugs through the IV line, I asked if there had been an attendant outside the hatch of the tank. Had the atmosphere been tested before he went in? Why wasn't there a ventilation system in place to provide him fresh outside air? Why wasn't a retrieval system attached to him? The man who identified himself as being in charge snapped at me and said, "What makes you an expert on confined tank work?

I said, "Sir, I am an OSHA confined space trainer and I know the laws about performing confined space work. You and

MEMOIRS OF MAYHEM

the others are negligent and it nearly cost this young man his life."

We transported our patient to the hospital where the ER staff continued to care for him. We retreated to the nurses' lounge where we documented our treatment on our patient care report. After cleaning and resupplying our rig, we handled another medical call and brought in another patient. After turning our patient over to the ER staff I walked to the nurses station and asked if the young man had regained consciousness. The charge nurse told me that he was and the endotracheal tube (ET) had been removed. I asked if it would be alright if I spoke with him for a moment before I left. She said that would be fine. I stepped into the treatment room and asked how he was feeling. He told me he had an excruciating headache and was sick to his stomach. I told him that was to be expected with the vapor concentration he had inhaled. The young man told me that he had taken a summer job working at the facility and was performing cleanup inside the tank at the direction of the supervisor.

I said, "Young man, you're not familiar with confined space entry work, but I am. I train people on the correct procedures and requirements to perform vessel work safely as required by law. They broke every rule in the book sending you into that tank and it could have cost you your life had they not found you when they did. I cannot say if you will have any longlasting health effects from this incident or not. When your parents arrive to take you home, I want you to tell them that for me. I also want you to tell them I said, 'Sue.'"

Chapter 37

CAN DREAMS FORETELL YOUR FUTURE?

I'VE NEVER BEEN one to put much credence in the contents of dreams. Most of us dream nearly every night, only to have forgotten them upon waking. But what about those few dreams that are as vivid as reality? those you can recall with perfect clarity upon waking or that even wake you from your sleep?

One night I dreamed that I was responding to a chest pain call. I was in the passenger seat; my partner had driving duty. Typically, we trade off driving after the conclusion of each call. In my dream we were approaching a signal light. As my partner approached the light, it changed from red to green giving us the right of way. He punched the accelerator and we charged into the intersection. I turned my head to the right and saw the grill of a semi-tractor about to impact the side of the ambulance. I woke up suddenly, my heart pounding. It took some time for me to shake the image from my mind so I could relax and go back to sleep.

The following morning, I prepared my duty bag with toiletries and change of clothes for my 24-hour shift and I met with my partner at our ambulance headquarters. We made shift change with the off-going crew members. We began the process of taking inventory and performing operational tests on equipment and checking all fluid levels in the engine compartment. With all pre-shift tasks completed, we drove to the gas station to top our fuel tank, then headed to our crew quarters which would serve as our overnight home. We parked the rig and plugged in the shoreline, which provided external power for the onboard heater to keep the interior at or about room temperature. We removed our duffel bags, went into our quarters, and performed a few menial housekeeping tasks while chatting about where we might have lunch later. We both stretched out on our beds, turned on the television set, and found a movie that we would enjoy. My partner soon fell asleep leaving me to watch the movie by myself.

About an hour had passed when our station phone rang. I grabbed it off the cradle and answered. Our dispatcher provided me an address and the nature of the call. I shouted to wake my partner and quickly jumped into my duty boots and ran to the door, grabbing the keys to the ambulance on my way out. My partner jumped into the passenger seat and we were on our way. When the dispatcher gave me the nature and location of the call, I realized that our route would take us through the intersection I had in my dream the previous night. A couple of minutes passed, when my partner inquired as to why I grabbed the keys when it was his turn to drive. I said, "I'll explain later."

Within minutes, we were approaching the traffic signal I had in my dream. There were no vehicles in our lane and the signal light was red. I slowly rolled toward the intersection; the light turned green. I made a complete stop just as a semi tractor trailer, with its air horn blaring, blew through the intersection against the red light. I quickly checked to ensure it was safe to proceed and continued. I then told my partner that I had a dream the night before, that he had driven into the path of the semi when the light changed on our way to a call.

He sank into his seat in silence and then replied, "I would have done the same thing under the circumstances."

I've shared this true story with many friends and relatives. The vast majority of those I have told about this, attribute this event as divine intervention, not luck or just a coincidence. When given a chance to see an event that could have ended my life, I took the steps necessary to change the outcome.

Chapter 38

―――∾∾∾―――

ANY LAST WORDS?

I WAS WORKING an ambulance one evening in a town not far from where I grew up. We heard that one of our units was called to a vehicle crash at the intersection of a state highway and a paved county road about fifteen miles away. Within just a couple of minutes, another crash occurred about six miles west of the first crash site. We got underway and headed in the direction of the second crash. We communicated with our unit on the first crash scene that we would need to get through their location to be able to get to the second crash in a timely manner. The crew told us that there would be no problem, just proceed with caution as we approached. We reduced our speed and approached slowly. We weaved our way through the emergency vehicles and sped our way to our scene a few miles down the road. The crash was at the intersection of two highways, one of which is a major truck route through Michigan. All of us working in emergency services were familiar with this area, as there had been several deadly incidents at this location over the years.

When we arrived, we saw that two vehicles were involved. It was apparent from looking at the cars as we approached that one had gone through the traffic signal striking the other in what we refer to as a T-bone collision; the vehicle had been crushed on its passenger side. Fire-rescue was on the scene setting up extrication tools. The driver's side door had been jammed on impact and the passenger side was crushed, so I sought an alternative to gain access to the injured man. I found the rear window had been blown out on impact. I crawled through the rear window opening, into the back seat, then up and over into the driver's seat.

In the front passenger seat was an elderly man having difficulty breathing. I identified myself and began a rapid patient survey. I determind his ribs were broken in multiple places. I was certain he had sustained serious internal injuries. The gentleman was ashen in color and was breathing in short, light breaths. I called for oxygen and placed an oxygen mask over his face. The fire department handed a blanket through the window to protect us from flying glass. I pulled the blanket over both our heads. I explained the sounds that he was hearing were the sounds of hydraulic tools that were being used to pry open the door. I held the oxygen mask on his face but he kept trying to remove it to speak to me. His spoke softly and with all the external noise I could barely hear him unless I placed my ear next to his face. In a few moments the rescue tools had succeeded in prying the door open and we were just ready to remove him when he expired.

I yelled, "Code blue!"

We hurriedly placed him on the gurney and loaded him into the ambulance. By pure coincidence, the owner of our ambulance service was dining a few miles away when he heard our call come in. He headed our way, arriving just as we were removing the victim from the wreckage. He said he would drive our rig, allowing both my partner and me to work on our patient. We did everything we could to save the man on the way to the hospital. Once we arrived, the ER staff continued resuscitative efforts for another fifteen minutes or so before pronouncing him. My partner and I slowly left the room, made our way outside, and began the process of cleaning the back of our unit to prepare it for the next call. When we were done, we went back inside to write up the transport report. We were both exhausted from our CPR efforts, lasting over twenty minutes, in the back of the bus.

I washed up and got a cup of coffee to sip while I wrote my report. As I was writing, a nurse came in and told me our patient's wife was in the lobby and wished to speak to me. I looked up and asked, "Does she know?"

She said "Yes! She has already been to the trauma room and seen her husband."

I told her that I would be right out. This was something I was not accustomed to nor prepared to do. It took some time before I gained the fortitude to face the grieving widow. I walked out into the lobby and saw an elderly lady standing next to the nurse's station. I introduced myself and she asked, "Did my husband have any last words before he passed?"

I could feel my throat getting tight as I prepared to get the words out. I swallowed and said, "Ma'am, we were in the car awaiting the extrication team to free us. I had his head cradled in my right elbow. I leaned forward so I could hear his voice over the hydraulic equipment being used. He took my left hand in his hand and he said to me, "Son, I've lived a good long life and I don't mind dying because I'm going to meet my Heavenly Father who's waiting for me. I just hope when it's your time to go that you're ready to meet Him too." With those words, he took a shallow breath, exhaled and was gone."

The response from this lady was nothing I could have imagined. She smiled and reached her frail little arms up and around my neck, gave me a hug and said, "Oh, that would be my sweet husband. You see, he is a retired minister and he was evangelizing to you with his last breath."

She thanked me for meeting with her and sharing her departed husband's last words. I turned away, went into the nurses' break room, grabbed a glass of water and sipped it to keep my airway from completely closing off. There have been times when my mind goes back to that night, and I can hear him speaking softly in the middle of the chaos.

Chapter 39

———✦———

UNRESPONSIVE SUBJECTS

ONE AFTERNOON, WHILE working a paramedic EMS unit, we were called to a residence for a report of an unresponsive subject. I've been called to many "unresponsive subject" calls over the years and they can run the gambit from diabetic emergencies, drug overdoses, alcohol intoxications, stroke, and cardiac arrests. With this type of call we never knew exactly what we're going to be dealing with. While responding, I would go over various scenarios and treatment protocols in my mind. We arrived, parked the rig in the driveway, grabbed our bags, walked to the door and knocked. A visibly upset elderly lady answered the door. I asked what the problem was in the home. She told us that she was unable to rouse her bedridden husband. She explained that he had asked her if she would go to a fast-food restaurant and pick up some lunch, as he was craving a burger, fries and chocolate shake. When she returned with the food, she was unable to waken him. I asked my partner to stay with the lady in the living room while I went to check on the husband. I walked through the very tidy, well-kept home and turned into the bedroom. The husband was lying on his back with his reading glasses in place. His eyes were motionless and I observed blood in the area of his temple. I moved from the foot of the bed around to the left side and saw a blue steel revolver lying on the floor near his outreached arm. I stepped around the gun, so as not to disturb it, leaned over and checked for a pulse. He had expired. As I stepped out of the room, I closed the door and walked back into the living room. I sat down beside the wife and before I could utter a word she looked up and said, "He's gone, isn't he?" I said softly, "Yes ma'am, I'm afraid he is". As she began to weep, my partner and I tried to console her. I asked my partner to step out of hearing range and I whispered to her what I had seen in the bedroom. She stayed with the wife while I placed a call to our dispatch center. I informed our dispatcher that we had an apparent suicide and would need police presence on the scene. Dispatch contacted the police department and we waited for officers to arrive. It was only three or four minutes before a police cruiser pulled in behind our unit. I explained to the officers what I had observed, assured them that nothing had been disturbed and that the wife was unaware that her husband had taken his own life. Apparently, he could no longer deal with being constricted to a bed, unable to enjoy mobility and quality of life. He lured her away from the home with his request for fast food. Once she had left, he was able to reach out with his right arm, open a nightstand drawer and remove the revolver. The couple had spent over fifty years together and sadly the marriage ended in an act of desperation and suicide.

We received a call one morning for a subject who had staggered into a convenience store and fell to the floor unconscious. My partner and I responded and arrived at the store, where we found a middle-aged man lying on the floor. As we obtained vital signs, we asked the manager how the patient was acting when he came through the door. He told us that the man was visibly staggering and holding onto the shelving as he made his way across the store. The man collapsed, pulling down a shelving unit as he fell. We began an IV line, placed him on 100 percent oxygen and hooked him up to a cardiac monitor. We injected medications though the IV line in accordance with protocol, which included a drug to counter the effects of narcotics. There was no response with the medications, so we placed him on our gurney and strapped him in for the trip to the emergency room. My partner called in his report of how the patient came into the store, what we had done with regard to treatment on the scene and a current set of his vital signs. When we arrived at the hospital's emergency room, they were ready for us. We quickly rolled him into one of the exam rooms and provided the ER staff assistance in transferring him from the gurney to the bed. The attending physician ordered arterial blood gases drawn for lab testing. An ABG is obtained when a needle is inserted into the wrist (typically) and blood is drawn from an artery within the wrist. When the blood was collected, the sample was rushed to the lab. In the interim, the ER staff continued to monitor the patient. My partner and I were busy getting our equipment back in order and changing out our drug box in the hospital pharmacy. The ER physician urgently called to us. He held the patient's driver's license in his hand and instructed us to get to his home address immediately. The doctor told us he had requested the fire department to perform a search of the patient's home. We responded to the address and found the fire department already on the scene. Within moments of our arrival, firefighters, wearing air tanks, carried our patient's wife out of the home. She was also unconscious. They found her lying in bed, still in her night clothes. We began treatment immediately and rushed her back to the hospital. Both the husband and wife had very high levels of carbon monoxide in their blood streams. Carbon monoxide is a colorless, odorless and tasteless gas, which kills approximately five hundred people each year, as a result of improperly ventilated appliances, engines or misuse of auxiliary heating systems in homes. Our attending physician had placed a call for a helicopter to transfer both patients to a hospital across the state which was equipped with a hyperbaric chamber. The hyperbaric chamber is pressurized to about three times normal atmospheric pressure to remove carbon monoxide from the hemoglobin. It was later determined that the couple had been grocery shopping the previous evening. During the process of carrying packages from the car into their home, the engine had been left running throughout the night as the pair slept. The vehicle was in an attached garage on the lower level of their home. The husband had left the home on foot to make the trip to the nearby convenience store. Both would fully recover from their near fatal event. Had it not been for the intuitiveness and quick actions on the part of our attending physician this incident would have had a deadly outcome.

Chapter 40

———∾∾———

IT'S IN YOUR BLOOD

ONE AFTERNOON WHEN I was the Emergency Management Coordinator, I closed up my office, went to the parking lot, and swept away the snow which had accumulated on my car. I got in and let my car warm up and un-fog the window before making my way home for dinner with my wife. The roadways were snow covered and slippery. I turned onto the main roadway heading out of town when I saw a pick-up truck begin to slide sideways and come across into the opposing lanes of traffic. I slowed and watched as the truck was struck by a car in front of me. I positioned my vehicle in the middle of the roadway in the turn lane and activated my hazard and emergency lights.

I got out with my first aid kit that I always carried with me and headed to the car. It had struck the sliding pick-up in the rear wheels, which caused the air bags to deploy. As I approached the car, I could hear screams.

I pulled the door open and a young lady inside yelled, "Get me out! Get me out! The car is on fire."

I took her hand and tried to calm her down and explained that the car was not on fire. I told her what she thought was smoke was in fact powder which is used as a lubricant to aid in the deployment of the airbags. I introduced myself and told her that I had served in the fire department for over twenty-five years. I asked her where she was hurt and she said she had sharp pains in her right lower leg. I raised myself from a stooped position where I could see her right leg resting against the floorboard. I saw that she had suffered a fracture above the ankle and her foot was turned inward ninety degrees from her leg. I told her that additional help was on the way and asked if she was having any neck or back pain, and she indicated that she was not. I told her to remain calm and not to move until the fire department and ambulance service arrived.

Shortly, a fire engine rolled in behind her crashed car. The fire captain in charge, whom I had known for many years, climbed down from his seat and walked over and said, "Do you miss running calls, Curt?"

I smiled and told him that I was an eyewitness and it happened right in front of me. He grinned and gave me a slap on my shoulder. I introduced the captain to the victim and informed her she was in good hands and they would take care of her. The EMS transport team was now on the scene and I told them she had a fractured right leg just above the ankle. Injuries of this nature are sometimes caused when a driver sees an imminent impact. They brace their legs against the floorboard or brake pedal. The force of impact breaks bones in the lower legs. A police officer approached me and asked me if I had witnessed the crash. I told him I had, so he asked me to tell him what I had seen and where I was when it occurred. He took down my statement, thanked me for my assistance and told me I could be on my way. I got in my car and headed home.

Later that evening, I received a phone call from my fire captain friend. He said, "Curt, the husband of the lady that was in the accident this afternoon wants to speak with you. I didn't feel comfortable providing him your phone number without your permission. I have his number if you would like to call him back."

I said, "Sure! Give me his number and I'll give him a call."

The lady's husband was out of state working on a project and couldn't be home with his wife who was undergoing corrective surgery on her leg, but he wanted to personally thank me for assisting his wife in her ordeal earlier in the day. He said when he spoke to his wife, she had been sedated but she told him the first guy who stopped to help her was Curtis, but he preferred Curt. She had also told him that he had previously been in the fire service and an EMT. He told her he would try to find me. He did so by contacting the fire department. He told me that his wife went on and on about how I had been able to calm her and explained what the fire department and EMS transport team would do when they arrived. I told him that it was a pleasure to assist his wife during this very traumatic event and that I hoped her surgery would be successful.

I had just taken delivery of a brand-new Harley Davidson touring bike in the spring some months later. I was at my home one Saturday morning when I got a call from a friend. He told me that he and another guy we ride with were heading to a large outdoor and sporting goods store and asked if I would ride over so they could take a look at my new ride. I grabbed my jacket and helmet and saddled up for the ride, which was only about twenty miles away. I met up with the guys in the parking lot and they congratulated me on my new ride. We visited for a while and I told them I needed to get back for some plans my wife and I had made.

As I pulled away from my friends, another rider pulled up and began engaging them in conversation. The man on the bike asked my friends if they knew a guy named Curtis. He told them he wanted to meet him in person because of what he had done for his wife. He told them that the guy used to be with the fire department but was now working in the office of emergency management.

My friend smiled and said, "Did you see the guy that just pulled out on the black Harley Ultra? That was him!"

He exclaimed, "You've got to be kidding me!" He asked my friends if they would provide him my address because he wanted to thank me personally. They provided him with my home address. A few days later, when I arrived home from my office, my wife told me he had stopped and delivered a bottle of wine as a token of his appreciation. A couple of months had passed when I rode to the local Harley dealership to pick up some cleaning supplies. I was visiting with a couple of guys outside the dealership when a couple rode up and got off their bike. The lady looked at me and broke into a big smile! She pointed her finger at me.

Her husband said, "That's Curtis isn't it?"

They walked over and gave me a friendly embrace. We got to know each other better and she told me about her recuperation and physical therapy. The take aways from this story are two fold: An act of kindness doesn't cost you anything, and don't stereotype bikers. There are a lot of nice people out there riding on two wheels.

Chapter 41

———— ∽∽∽ ————

ALL HANDS ON DECK

WHILE WORKING IN my office, during my years with the county, I received a call from the dispatch center. I was told that a large plastic recycling center was on fire, burning out of control. Three fire departments were either on the scene or heading to the scene. I responded across town and could see a column of thick black smoke rising skyward. I arrived on scene and sought out the officer in charge who was busily engaged in getting fire apparatus into position and summoning additional resources. I contacted dispatch and requested the county mobile command center be brought to the area of the fire. The command center allows those in charge a quiet place to discuss strategic planning, away from all the activity and onlookers. When the unit arrived, I sought to find a power supply so that the radio equipment and the air conditioning would have power. Eventually, the officer in charge came to me and asked if I had a copy of the county mutual aid box alarm system (MABAS) with me. *

All of my reference materials were already in the command center. He opened the book, grabbed the radio, and requested a second box alarm, which would bring an additional four fire departments to the scene. The city maintenance staff had placed barricades around several blocks to prevent traffic from getting close to the scene. I placed a call to the Department of Environmental Quality to notify them of the fire and then notified the Emergency Management & Homeland Security Division of the Michigan State Police what was taking place.** We staffed the command center with the police chief, fire officer in charge, city maintenance supervisor, a representative from city government, and myself. A local college campus, radio stations, and area businesses were notified of a shelter-in-place around the city due to the presence of the heavy potentially toxic smoke. Door-to-door evacuations in the immediate area had been performed by members of local law enforcement. A third box alarm was requested, bringing even more resources to the scene. As with many emergencies, media representatives rushed to the scene to obtain information.

I stepped outside to see how things were going, when media representatives called to me. I went over to where they had gathered and they asked me for an update on the situation. I told them that I would not provide them a statement; any statement would come from the fire officer in charge of the scene. I informed them that I would speak to him and relay their request. About ten minutes later, the officer came into the command center and I told him that the media asked for an update. He begrudgingly said, "Alright, but I need you outside."

We walked out and he handed me his radio and said, "You're temporarily in charge of the scene while I'm tied up."

I pressed the transmit button and notified everyone on the scene of the change in command. When the media conference was completed, the fire officer regained charge over the incident. He asked, "What am I missing?"

I replied, "Well, the engines on the trucks have been running at full throttle for nearly two hours and they will need fuel soon."

"Can you take care of that for me?" he asked.

I said, "You bet."

I walked to the command center, opened my resource book, called a fuel delivery service, and ordered a truckload of diesel fuel to resupply the fire trucks. Within a few minutes the fuel truck was making its way around the scene, topping off the fuel tanks of all the trucks engaged on the scene. Fire apparatus would be on the scene throughout most of the day before being released and sent back to their respective stations. In total, firefighters and trucks from thirteen agencies were involved in the suppression efforts. It was a very long day for everyone involved.

*Mutual Aid Box Alarm Systems provides a rapid deployment of resources for large emergencies when an agency, jurisdiction or region is stricken by an overwhelming event; see MABAS.

** One of the many responsibilities of a county Emergency Management Coordinator is to push information to the state level to provide them a situational awareness of major emergencies occurring across the state.

Chapter 42

Chapter 42

FATAL CHEMISTRY

WORKING IN MY office as the Emergency Management Coordinator, I received a phone call from our 911 call center director. He said one of our police chiefs had come upon a vehicle in a community park outside the edge of his city. The chief could see a subject behind the wheel of the car. He said when he got out of his patrol car to do a welfare check, he smelled a pungent odor coming from inside the car. The police chief reported that he thought the subject in the vehicle was deceased. I told the director to relay to the chief that no one was to go near the vehicle. I suspected the car was filled with a deadly poisonous gas and I was on the way to the scene. The 911 director acknowledged and said he would get the message delivered.

I headed to the chief's location. When I arrived on the scene, I met with him and told him my suspicions. "I think the individual has mixed chemicals together which produced a deadly mixture." The fire department had already arrived and the newly formed county hazardous materials team had been requested to the scene. As we waited for everyone to arrive, I put an action plan together which would utilize the hazardous material response team and it's equipment. When everyone was on site, I called for a meeting to discuss the step-by-step process on how we would go about mitigating the incident.

Access to the park had been blocked off to prevent the general public from entering. I told everyone that nothing we could do was going to change the outcome for the person in the car. We would take our time, move slowly and deliberately to make sure that everyone on the site remained safe. The first objective was to have two firefighters suit up in SCBA (self-contained breathing apparatus), approach the vehicle, and perform reconnaissance to identify the chemicals involved. The firefighters suited up, approached the vehicle, looked inside the car, came back out and reported their findings. I contacted the state police operations center to verify that the two chemicals identified inside the vehicle formed a deadly gas. Step two of the process was to have the doors of the vehicle opened up and step away, allowing the gases trapped inside the car to dissipate into the outside air. The car was left alone for about fifteen minutes with fire department ventilating fans pushing air through the vehicle. I asked the local fire chief if he had any sodium bicarbonate. He didn't, so he called his station and requested five boxes of baking soda and a few wooden paint stir sticks brought to the scene. A while later, a firefighter arrived on scene with the requested materials.

We had firefighters retrieve the pail from the vehicle, carry it carefully back, and place it on the ground. I instructed the firemen to slowly add the baking soda, blend it into the contents, and continue the process until the liquid became a thick paste. I cautioned them that the neutralizing process could generate heat if added too quickly. The container was neutralized safely without incident. A makeshift table served as a decontamination area for the deceased. The victim was carried to the table, his body and clothing were washed and scrubbed to remove any residual contaminants, then the body placed in a shroud for transportation. The clothing, pails, and miscellaneous items from the vehicle were placed in a hazardous waste container for incineration. Before the car was removed from the site, firefighters used hoses from their fire engine to flush out the entire interior of the vehicle. Although this type of incident had previously occurred in other parts of the country, this was the first reported case in the state at the time. Once again, our first responders showed great teamwork in mitigating this incident. If the police chief or an innocent citizen had opened the door and leaned inside the car, it could have resulted in further loss of life.

Chapter 43

———— ∞ ————

HAZARDOUS MATERIAL TANKER CRASH

SHORTLY AFTER 2:00 p.m. one Monday afternoon, I received a call from our dispatch center informing me of a vehicular crash on a state highway involving a tanker truck. I was told that an overturned tanker truck was leaking chemicals. I hung up the phone, got into my car and responded to the scene. I notified the Michigan State Police operations center from my car. I would provide them an update when I arrived on the scene. While listening to the fire service and police radio traffic on the way, a request had been sent for additional agencies to report to the scene, including a medical helicopter. I arrived and found that a car had been struck when it pulled out in front of a tanker truck. The semi tractor/tanker had rolled over during the collision. I was told that the leaking contents were acetone. Acetone is a very volatile and flammable chemical and has numerous applications, such as a paint component, varnishes, thinning polyester resins, and nail polish removers.

The driver of the car had expired on impact and the tanker driver was pinned in the truck wreckage with critical injuries. The fire department was working feverishly to extricate him, when a helicopter arrived and hovered overhead. The fire department had previously closed the highway and the medical chopper was cleared to land on the highway a short distance from the wreckage. Unfortunately, just as the flight team arrived, the truck driver succumbed to his injuries. When police agencies arrived, they took control of blocking and rerouting traffic around the crash site. A total of five fire departments had apparatus and personnel on the scene, as well as a two county hazardous materials team had been called in to assist with the dangerous operations. * The incident commander requested loads of dirt to be brought to the scene as a way of creating a dam in the embankment to contain the leaking chemical so it didn't contaminate property away from the incident scene. Fire retardant foam was applied around and on the tanker to prevent a flash fire. Within an hour of the incident, media representatives had arrived on the scene.

I alerted the incident commander that the media was requesting an update. He asked me to go handle their questions. I provided the media information regarding two fatalties, the chemical leaking from the tanker, and that there would be a very lengthy highway closure while local fire departments and Haz Mat teams worked to mitigate the incident. The law enforcement officers created a bypass around the scene to allow traffic to flow back onto the state highway. Over the next several hours, another tanker truck would be brought in, and a pump was connected between the two tankers. They slowly began to offload the chemical into the replacement tanker. The process was tedious, which made it late into the evening before the everything had been completed. When the replacement tanker containing the chemical had cleared the scene, large wreckers were brought in to upright the overturned tanker and the semi-tractor. The highway was reopened to traffic sometime after eleven o'clock that evening.

Two lives were lost in the incident, which was tragic, but the potential of what could have happened would have been a much larger disaster. I was proud of our first responders, police, fire, and EMS members as they worked together to deal with a very precarious situation that day. After the incident, I received a phone call from the fire chief in charge of the operation and he asked me if I would serve as the facilitator for a post-incident critique he was planning. I told him I would be glad to do that for him. Every agency involved in the incident was invited to take part. Two weeks later, the meeting took place in a large hall with representatives from all the fire departments. This included two hazardous materials responce teams, law enforcement officers, EMS providers, state department of transportation, Michigan State Police Emergency Management and wrecker operators. The meeting lasted nearly two hours and was highly constructive. It covered each aspect of the very delicate and complicated scene that took part that night.

*A hazardous material team is an organized group who have specialized training and equipment to deal with hazardous materials incidents. Hazardous materials are categorized by the US Department of Transportation and additional information about specific classifications of hazardous materials can be found at fmcsa.dot.gov

Chapter 44

———⚬⚬⚬———

A Mission of Mercy

MY WIFE, WHO is a registered nurse, was contacted by a medical missions group and asked if she would consider making another trip to Guatemala. This is a group of medical professionals who provides care for the natives in a remote part of the country. My wife had previously worked on this medical relief group before we were married. She told her friend that she was interested but wouldn't go unless I could go with her. The friend asked her what skills I had that would make me useful to the team. My wife explained to him that I had worked in Emergeny Medical Services for many years and could perform most any task that an RN could do. The organizers with HELPS International agreed that I could be included on the medical team.

A couple of months would pass before it was time to make our journey. In the interim, I needed to get up to date with inoculations required for international travel. We flew from Detroit to Guatemala City. We were bused to a remote part of the country in the mountains with military escorts in front of and behind us, armed with machine guns. However, the presence of these armed men did not particularly provide me a warm fuzzy feeling about my decision. The team of forty-five consisted of surgeons, ophthalmologists, anesthesiologists, pharmacists, dentists, registered nurses, translators, cooks, and a couple of guys who were jokingly referred to as MacGyvers—they had skills for repairing most anything we might encounter.

All of the surgical equipment, pharmaceuticals, hospital scrubs, medical supplies, food, and water were taken with us to the hospital. We arrived at the building, located in a mountainous area, that would serve as a working hospital. We off-loaded all our equipment and began the process of sweeping, cleaning, and sanitizing the building for use. When everything had been cleaned, we began removing the supplies from their containers and setting up a surgical prep area, two surgical suites, a surgical step-down (post-op) unit, cafeteria, and our sleeping quarters. All surgical instruments were sterilized in an autoclave unit.

After two days of preparation we were ready to receive patients. Many of the people who were in need of medical care were already lined up outside our compound, which was surrounded by high fencing with only one gate for access. All patients were interviewed and triaged by our translators. Everyone was assigned a twelve-hour shift. My wife was assigned to work with one of the doctors and I was given the task of working in the surgical recovery unit. The RN in charge of the unit didn't have a particular liking for me, because I was not a nurse. My responsibilities were to walk around the unit, take and record sets of vitals periodically, and report any patient that was having acute reactions or experiencing signs of distress from the procedure they had received.

On the second evening, a doctor came into the cafeteria and sat down at my table. He said, "I'm hearing a lot of rumors about you and your years of experience working in the pre-hospital setting."

I said, "Yes sir, I've worked advanced life support units for several years."

He replied, "I suppose you've seen some pretty nasty things during that time."

I assured him that I had indeed. He asked me if I had ever witnessed an autopsy, I told him that I had seen a few. He asked me if I had any problems with them. I told him, "No, I did not." I said, "Doc, I'm not sure where you're going with this conversation, but I can assure you that over the course of working fire-rescue and ambulance services I have witnessed the human body disassembled in many ways."

He replied, "Well, I could use another set of hands in surgery in the morning and wondered if you were up to the task?"

"What time shall I scrub up?"

The surgeon responded, "I have a patient with a very large tumor in her belly and I have scheduled her for surgery at ten o'clock."

I told him that I would be there ready to assist him. The next morning, I told the charge nurse that I would be assisting in surgery at ten and would not be available for a while. She told me that they would cover my opening until I returned. I left the recovery unit and made my way to the surgical suite to scrub up. I stepped into the surgical room where a nurse applied my gloves, gown, mask, and head cover. I walked to the operating table, taking a position next to the surgeon. He thanked me for my willingness to assist him. They brought in the patient, who had already been put to sleep with a drug administered through an IV line. The anesthesiologist placed an endotracheal tube in place and connected it to a mechanical ventilator. Cardiac monitoring patches were put in place to observe her vital signs throughout the surgery. The surgeon applied a solution to cleanse the patient's abdomen and scrubbed the entire area to remove bacteria. Using a scalpel, he made an incision from the bottom of the chest bone down to the pubic area. Retractors were used to expose the abdominal cavity. With the abdminal cavity opened, I could see the tumor. It was about the size of a large grapefruit. The surgeon instructed me to grasp the tumor and gently move it for him as he directed. We were standing shoulder to shoulder as he instructed me to shift up or down, left or right, as he delicately removed fingerlings from the tumor which had attached themselves to other structures within the abdominal cavity.

At one point, he said, "I think you're being spied on."

I said, "Sir?"

He whispered, "Check out your nine o'clock position."

I looked over my left shoulder and saw my wife taking pictures from a window located in the adjoining scrub room. When the surgeon gave me the word, I removed the tumor and placed it in a large stainless bowl for later examination. The procedure lasted about an hour. The patient was sutured, antibacterial solution applied and a dressing was placed over the incision. The surgeon later thanked me and said I did a great job assisting in the procedure. It gave me a good feeling that I played a small part in saving the life of the Guatemalan lady.

The following day in the post-operative unit, the charge

nurse, an elderly lady, who had served as a nursing school instructor, walked up to me with her hands resting on her hips and asked, "Do you EMS type people know how to use Foley catheters?"

I smiled and replied, "Why yes, ma'am, we do."

She explained that a man in bed five had not urinated since his surgery the previous day and needed a catheter. I told her I'd be happy to do that. With the assistance of a translator, I went to his bedside, pulled portable curtains around the bed, and told the translator what I was about to do and why. She translated the message to the man. The catheter was inserted and cuff inflated, at which time he nearly filled the collection bag. Mission accomplished! I'm sure the patient appreciated having a male do the procedure instead of a female nurse.

Later in the day, one of the surgeons came to me and asked, "How about you coming to the surgical waiting room in the morning and starting all the IV's for our scheduled surgery patients before you start your rounds in recovery? We're tying up a lot of our surgical nurses' time prepping patients when we could be performing more procedures."

I told him I would be glad to do that and I would be there the following morning. I arrived bright and early and went around the room, patient to patient, hanging bags of fluid, flushing the IV tubing and starting IV's on all those who would have surgical procedures performed that day. I continued each morning prior to starting my shift in the surgical step-down unit.

One morning while working in post-op, I heard screams coming from the far end of the hallway. A nurse yelled, "Doctor, Doctor!" She came flying through the door pushing a wheelchair. A lady had lapsed into unconsciousness as she was about to be released.

I scooped the little lady up, carried her to an empty bed, and laid her down. I turned to the nurses gathered around. I said, "I want 100% oxygen administered and two IV lines started." I went to the foot of the bed and lifted and locked it into an inverted position, while a nurse obtained her blood pressure and heart rate.

Within a few minutes, the lady started coming around just as a doctor walked into the room. He asked, "What's going on here?" The nurse who had rushed her down the hall explained to the doctor that the patient had passed out while being discharged. The doctor asked for a current set of vitals and nodded his head. He said, "OK, we've got 100% oxygen being administered, the bed is in Trendelenburg [inverted, feet higher than the head], bilateral IV lines running and a good set of vitals. It seems we are good here, so I'll head back to surgery now."

The nurses all stood there staring at me. I said, "Ladies, we deal with shock on a daily basis in the prehospital setting."

We all returned to our respective jobs. The patient was released later that day in good condition. A few days later it was time for us to leave. However, a glitch had developed before we could depart. A teacher's strike was taking place and the airport was being blocked by demonstrators. United States airline carriers had halted all flights in and out of the county as a result. A private charter was secured. We loaded a bus and went around the backside of the airport and entered through the Guatemalan air force base. Armed military personnel came on board and checked each of our passports before we were permitted entry into the base. We made our way across the airport runway to a hangar where a private aircraft was waiting for us. The owner of the aircraft was there. I approached him and asked, "Is this aircraft large enough to get us back to the United States?"

He replied, "You're not going to the United States. You're all going to El Salvador!"

I didn't know a lot about El Salvador, but what I did know was not very good! We loaded all our baggage into the cargo hold and climbed aboard the plane, which flew us to San Salvador. Our aircraft was the only flight landing at the airport that evening and the airport was closed. A large flat-bed truck pulled up alongside of our aircraft and we unloaded our equipment under the watchful eyes of military personnel holding machine guns. We spent the night at a luxurious five-star hotel. An American carrier picked us up to take us back to the United States the following day. It was a very eventful ending to our trip. It was gratifying and humbling to have taken part in helping the indigenous people in Guatemala, knowing that our team had extended and saved several lives that would have been lost had we not been there to intervene. The team organizers thanked my wife and me for our contributions during the mission. I had broken through a barrier. Never before had a prehospital care provider taken part in one of their mission trips. The organizers asked me if I had any EMS friends that might be interested in taking part in future trips.

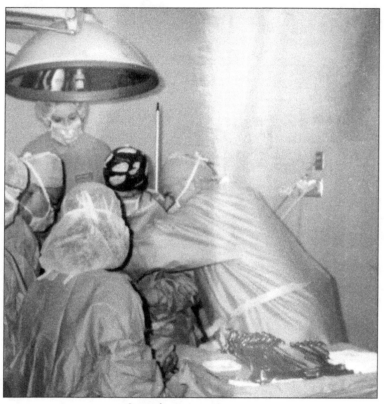

Surgical team removing tumor

ACKNOWLEDGEMENTS

My thanks to my wife, Gail and Brother-In-Law, John Myers and others for planting the seed and encouragement to write about my life stories. Writing a book is something that I would have never considered otherwise. To my Children, Jennifer, Curtis, and Brandon, I know there were times I missed events and family gatherings due to my working two jobs at times. For that I apologize, but I always tried to provide for you as best I could. I hope that you can forgive me.

I have been honored and blessed to have worked with some of the finest professionals over the years. I choose not to list you by name in fear of leaving someone out, but you all know who you are! Having worked for four private ambulance services in three different counties, as well as a fire department-based ALS system, I have gained numerous friendships that I will always cherish. I have worked with the finest EMTs and Paramedics anywhere in the country and learned so much from you along the way. We've seen and shared so much together. Thanks for the memories and the privilege of riding along. I will never forget you.

To the members of the law enforcement community, City, Township, County and the State of Michigan, thank you for your support, your friendship, but most of all, your dedication to serving our communities and its' citizens. Thank you for having our backs in the street and know that you will always have my support.

To all the health care providers I have worked with over the years, emergency room physicians, nurses, and technicians, I thank you for your dedication and for doing everything within your power to ease the pain and suffering of patients under your care. I am proud to have been able to work with you all and salute you for what you do on a daily basis. Public safety, emergency services and health care may be fundamentally different in nature, however, they all share one common core value; to make things better for those they serve.

I have studied under some great instructors who taught me the skills to perform the tasks required of me in the field. They not only provided skill sets, but also taught ethics and instilled a sense of purpose to do the very best for the lives of our citizens. I am fortunate to have played a small part in affecting the lives of those whose paths I've crossed over the years. It was my privilege to do so.

CPSIA information can be obtained
at www.ICGtesting.com
Printed in the USA
BVHW031100220421
605632BV00008B/871

9 781977 233394